EROSION OF AUTHORITY

EROSION OF
AUTHORITY

edited and with an introduction by
CLYDE L. MANSCHRECK

ABINGDON PRESS
nashville   ●   new york

EROSION OF AUTHORITY

Copyright © 1971 by Abingdon Press

ISBN 0-687-11996-0

Library of Congress Catalog Card Number: 72-134244

SET UP, PRINTED, AND BOUND BY THE
PARTHENON   PRESS,   AT   NASHVILLE,
TENNESSEE, UNITED STATES OF AMERICA

CONTENTS

AUTHORITY AND SKEPTICISM: AN INTRODUCTORY ESSAY

clyde l. manschreck

Few problems plague modern man more than the problem of authority. It touches every aspect of man's life whether he is conscious of it or not. On practical as well as theoretical levels—in religion, economics, politics, and social affairs—the problem of authority pervades everything that we do. Even the apparent lack of authority seems to increase rather than decrease the problem—in the political sphere giving rise to license, anarchy, and terror and, by way of reaction, to varied forms of totalitarianism. The basis on which one determines that anarchy is better or worse than tyranny, or uncon-

trolled freedom better or worse than rigid con-
formity, is also a matter of authority. Differences
regarding authority underlie confrontations, judgments, revolutions, criticisms, and wars. According
to what standard or authority shall this or that be
done and why? By what authority did John Calvin
condemn Servetus, or Dietrich Bonhoeffer attempt
to assassinate Hitler? By what authority do the
Black Panthers and other minority groups defy the
government? By what authority are American military forces entitled to kill the Viet Cong, or hippies
to opt out of society? By what authority are priests
attempting to alter the rule of enforced celibacy?
To examine the basis on which these matters rest
is to encounter the many faces of the elusive but
ever-present reality of authority. Whether one lives
by the *via negativa* of mysticism, the social activism
of a Dr. Spock, the indifference of Camus' *The
Stranger*, or the domination of a Mao, he is involved
in authority. Broadly speaking, authority refers to
the guidelines that prevail in our lives.

These guidelines can be internal or external, accepted voluntarily or imposed. They can be hidden
or open, expressed or unexpressed, temporary or
permanent, and in everyday life are likely to be a
combination of these, but they are always there.
Synonyms for authority might be standards, idols,

ideals, principles, loyalties; the forms of authority are manifold: government, law, dogma, tyranny, power, selfishness, individualism, and socialism, to name only a few.

But such aspects of authority have always been a part of human life. What is there about authority that makes it such a vital question today?

The answer is complex, yet one ingredient seems to emerge: authority is an especially significant question today because in our time we are witnessing a collapse of agreement on values without which authority, other than that imposed by sheer force, seems to be impossible. What agreement is there on social goals? What is true? What is good? What is beautiful? The answers vary from individual to individual, from country to country, from ethnic group to ethnic group. Even for the same individual the answers might well change from day to day. In the past, even though philosophers, theologians, and politicians differed, philosophy, theology, and politics provided acceptable guidelines for Western man, but today all three are being doubted.[1] Skepticism has propelled us into uncertainty and perplexity. Even science is viewed with a jaundiced

[1] See *Freedom and Community*, by Yves R. Simon, ed. Charles P. O'Donnell (New York: Fordham University Press, 1968), p. xvii.

eye because special interests so often color its conclusions.

In the first volume of the Nomos series, Dr. Carl J. Friedrich argues with great cogency that authority must have as its basis the potentiality of being reasonably elaborated.[2] It is not necessary that all commands, judgments, and actions be actually elaborated, but it is necessary that people *believe* that they can be reasonably elaborated in terms of the values, opinions, and views generally accepted, contends Dr. Friedrich. Otherwise authority loses its basis, for authority is not simply sheer power. A rational basis or component is crucial in authority, and when that component deteriorates, authority deteriorates.[3] Dr. Friedrich's thesis is a sound one, except for one thing; modern man has become acutely conscious that there is no absolute truth that *reason* can validate—a metaphysical truism which renders relative all conclusions about authority based on reason. Dr. Friedrich recognizes this situation at the end of his essay when he says that constitutional order can be maintained only if man retains a sense of obliga-

[2] "Authority, Reason, and Discretion," in *Authority*, ed. Carl J. Friedrich (Cambridge: Harvard University Press, 1958), pp. 28-48.
[3] *Ibid.*, p. 39.

tion with regard to the potentiality of reasoned elaboration. "Once this regard is lost—and it may be lost by man at large no longer accepting reason as a guide—the night of meaningless violence is upon us." [4] That night of meaningless violence would appear to be falling at the present time. If reasonable elaboration is the crux of the problem of authority and if such elaboration is only relatively possible, then authority has no firm basis, this in turn may well manifest itself in anarchy and terror currently seen in college disruption, riots, street violence, and increased rates of crime. Reason is no longer accepted as a final guide because reason is so often corrupted by self-interest. The objective method, for example, (never attainable in any pure sense) is now being radically questioned even as an *ideal* for research, despite the fruits that it has yielded in scholarship. We look in vain for any unifying consensus on the undergirding values that make social living possible.[5] So, while almost all the major aspects of authority have been discussed by great thinkers in the past—Aristotle, Hobbes,

[4] *Ibid.,* p. 39.

[5] See "Authority and Freedom in Modern Western Democracy" by Wilhelm Geiger in *Freedom and Authority in the West,* ed. George N. Shuster (Notre Dame, Ind.: University of Notre Dame Press, 1967), p. 64.

Hooker, Rousseau, Hume, Kant, Aquinas—the question of authority is vital in the twentieth century in a peculiar way because historical developments have brought about a climate of opinion in which there are no universally acceptable standards of values. Ambiguity reigns. There may not even be a valid moral order, such as thinkers in the past envisaged, certainly no moral order that is recognizable and equally binding for all.[6]

This rejection or radical questioning of values lies at the heart of the development that has brought about our crisis of authority. Skepticism has been common in the West, but the epistemological subjectivism that permeates the present situation is peculiarly widespread and virulent. It makes all statements of value highly relative. Without an agreement on ultimate standards to which all can appeal, common goals become almost impossible. Every person seems bent on "doing his thing" whether it be creative art, environmental violence, sexual permisiveness, enlarging the gross national product, or drug tripping—as if boundless license is the one essential ingredient of life. One might assume that to have any viable kind of society individuals would have to accept an obligation to

[6] *Ibid.*, pp. 64-65.

12

protect and care for one another. But this is not self-evident. Some question whether society should be protected, for society in the eyes of some radicals has become such a mess that even sudden nuclear destruction is welcome as a means of ending it. Increasingly widespread bombings are a step in this direction. Thus nihilism with its aura of meaninglessness, chaos, indifference and death, intrudes into the situation, further eroding any basis for authority. In considering authority we can ill afford to ignore the nihilistic observations of such men as Albert Camus, Samuel Beckett, and Jean-Paul Sartre, for they are articulating a pervasive condition in our society. We are overcome by doubts concerning the meaning of life and find ourselves with no commonly accepted principles for individual and social living. Albert Camus has given this condition shocking expression in his essays on "Absurd Reasoning," "The Absurd Man," and "Absurd Creation." Everything is absurd, without purpose, without meaning. We are like Sisyphus who was condemned to push a rock up a hill, only to watch it roll down again and repeat the performance—endlessly.[7] To no purpose, we, too, push rocks up the hill.

[7] *The Myth of Sisyphus and Other Essays* (New York: Vintage Books, Random House, 1955), pp. 1-91.

Without agreement on values, goals, and purposes, a logical assumption is that social cohesion, if we are to have a viable society, has to be imposed externally. Yet the same erosion of values occasioned by radical subjective relativism has already undercut the two institutions that have been most visible in the imposition of authority in the life of Western man—the church and the state. For centuries these two institutions vied with each other for control of society. The state finally displaced the church as the dominant institution, but is today itself in jeopardy of being displaced. Church and state have both fulfilled needed functions, but both have fallen into the demonic pride of absolute authoritarianism, which history has a way of exposing as pretense. Men have rejected that pretense in the case of the church; they are in the turmoil of rejecting it in the case of the state, and this conflict has heightened the crisis of authority, for what will replace the state is not yet apparent.

After the persecuted Christian Church of the early centuries joined forces with Emperor Constantine in 313, as a result of the Edict of Milan, the church for the first time had the physical means to implement its sovereign claims. Before the end

14

of the fourth century, Christianity had become the only legal religion in the Roman Empire and by 416 only Christians could serve in the army. Even though ecclesiastical sovereignty was never complete and often shaky, still political circumstances and sacerdotal sacramentalism enabled the church to gain general control of society in the Middle Ages. The confrontation of pope and king at Canossa in 1077, the crusades, the control of Europe from London to Constantinople under Pope Innocent III, and the Inquisition in Spain and the Netherlands in the fifteenth and sixteenth centuries symbolize this ecclesiastical domination of society. During the Middle Ages those who dared to abrogate papal dictums were summarily excommunicated, exiled, deprived of property, imprisoned, or executed. Torture was authorized in 1252 to make people confess and conform, and the inquisition under Torquemada and Ximenes operated with almost no regard for human rights. Ironically, a theology of love (so brilliantly depicted in Dostoievsky's Grand Inquisitor)[8] undergirded all this activity.

However, men came to doubt the papal claim to

[8] *The Brothers Karamazov,* trans. Constance Garnett (Modern Library; New York: Random House, n.d.), Bk. V, chap. v.

15

truth and for a variety of motivations to resist the proximate and ultimate goals of the keepers of "God's revelation." Scripture and tradition prevailed as generally accepted authorities in the early church and medieval period, with the pope at Rome emerging as the sovereign interpreter of both. Rome's direct tie with Christ through Peter and Paul (the Apostolic Succession) gave the Roman bishop an added edge of authority over churches that could claim none or only one apostolic link, especially after the destruction of Jerusalem in 70 and again in 135. This position was not seriously questioned during the Middle Ages, so that Rome could and did assert authority over spiritual and secular matters. Boniface VIII's *Unam Sanctam* in 1302, claiming supreme authority for the pope, and his introduction of the triple tiara on the papal crown to show the rule of Father, Son, and Holy Spirit through the pope, are historical symbols of the sovereign stance of the papacy. Thomas Aquinas elaborated this ecclesiastical sovereignty in his famous *Summa*, one of the few truly great theological statements in Western culture, weaving together both reason and faith. Yet the medieval synthesis began to crack, for men began to question the basic claims. Significantly, nominalism, which

16

maintained that overarching values such as justice, beauty, goodness and truth were mere names, had much to do with the weakening of ecclesiastical sovereignty. To the ordinary man the self-serving worldliness of the church seemed to be no more justified than that of other groups. Gradually the nations of Europe began to assert their own national sovereignties. Changing economic, political, and social developments, along with an epistemological erosion of formerly accepted truths, prompted ethnic groups to assert themselves and usher in the period of national sovereignty, a period in which a pluralism of nations prevailed, each one acting as if it were absolute, each one serving its own interests.

Martin Luther is significant from this perspective because he successfully challenged and overtly shattered the sovereignty of the papacy. He proclaimed the Bible and justification by faith alone, principles strong enough to break the authoritarian structure of the church, but not that of the state. The exigencies of the times pressed Luther to appeal to the secular powers for support. An alliance resulted that left the state in control of both religion and education, a situation dramatized on the 450th anniversary of the birth of Luther when the bishops of Germany hailed Hitler as a savior sent to them by God.[9]

In the wake of the Middle Ages the problem of sovereignty was not solved; man merely traded the sovereignty of the church for a plurality of sovereign states. The end of the Thirty Years' War (1618–1648) is sometimes said to mark the end of the church-state struggle for sovereignty, for that war, ostensibly between the Protestants and Catholics, marks the last great conflict in Western culture fought mainly over religion. When it ended, the pope pronounced the treaty "null and void" because so little attention had been given to his claims, but his voice went virtually unheeded. Even though infallibility was dogmatized at Vatican Council I in 1870, the power of the church as the organizing authority for society has steadily declined. However, the papacy has not officially disclaimed its primacy over spiritual and secular affairs, and did not, until 1966, abolish the office of the inquisition.

The Anabaptists of the sixteenth century and the

[9] See documents in *The German Phoenix,* by Franklin Littell (New York: Doubleday & Co., 1960) and "Relations between Church and State in Europe," by Peter Meinhold in *Freedom and Authority in the West,* ed. George N. Shuster, pp. 41-53, for a general discussion of the church-state situation.

free church groups afterward generally rejected the sovereignty of both the church and the state, leaving us with a legacy of individual sovereignty in that every man decides voluntarily what his ultimate trust will be. This contributed to a development of toleration, but other forces were necessary to bring about a serious questioning of the sovereignty of the state. These were the growing forces of skepticism, subjective relativism, and nihilism.

Science and technology from the seventeenth century to the present have made men increasingly conscious of their ability to manipulate the forces of nature. And rationalism has enabled men to shake the remaining shackles of ecclesiasticism. But in the course of the centuries men have lost not only a sense of the transcendent, but also a trust in reason, for reason is finite and subjective, and cannot therefore establish ultimate values. This leaves man with relativism: A thing is true or good according to the stance of the observer, so that all of man's knowing and valuing are permeated with subjective relativism. No final authority can be validated. Even the common man has come to recognize this, and this has given each man's own conclusions a dignity and status unparalled in our Western development. Pushed to its radical con-

clusion, however, such relativism leaves man with
no final standard to which he can appeal for
authority. In theory there are as many standards
as there are individuals.

The French Revolution in 1789 did as much
as anything else to make the world aware of relativism, to shatter old authorities. Behind it was a
century or more of rationalistic probing and questioning of the bases of the mores of authority.
When the Revolution erupted, it shattered old
political forms and cried out in violence and frustration that every man's view of what is good has as
much right to be recognized as any other. Its effects
reverberated throughout the world. The authority
of the state could no longer be assumed to be
sacrosanct. Who is to say what shall be given final
authority? If a portion of society suffers injustice,
is not something wrong?

That the sovereign authority of the state is being
profoundly questioned in our own day may be seen
especially in the ferment among Blacks and on
college campuses, among young people who are
keenly aware of the relativism of all truths. The
militant American Black recognizes that when
Whites talk about law and order they are talking
about something beneficial to the Whites, for
American law and order has its constitutional

foundations in a society that accepted slavery and, for representational purposes, regarded the slave as only 3/5 of a person. Consequently, relative White justice marks the legal codes erected on such a basis. The Black unrest in this country and in other lands is in part, at least, an effort to make this situation evident and to alter it. Authority on such a basis is clearly not acceptable to Blacks.

Many young people are in ferment, not only in his country but in England, France, Germany, Japan, and China. Chauvinistic nationalism has come to have an empty ring, a hollow appeal. An ideal of man as man, an assertion of humanity as such, regardless of geographic boundaries and racial colorations, is being asserted. While there have always been protests to war and the refusal of many to serve in the armed forces, today these have a different overtone. Thousands of young Americans are fleeing to Canada, Sweden, and Austria rather than be drafted to wage a war that they judge to be immoral and illegal. Others are going to jail, taking alternative service, or declaring conscientious objection. Still others do not register because they do not want to cooperate even that much with an establishment which they regard as corrupt and unjust. This is not a lack of love of country. Rather, as in the case of ecclesiastical

21

sovereignty, national sovereignty is being rejected because it is not regarded as ultimate. The questioning of national sovereignty is the added overtone. An immediate impetus for this stance came undoubtedly from the Nuremberg trials, which did not allow Nazis to use obedience to authority as a justification for commiting atrocities. Moral responsibility was laid upon the individual. The My Lai incident in Vietnam, if regarded as an individual responsibility or if regarded as the product of military activity, may well boomerang on the sovereignty of the state and its military authority— in the one case because of the principle of individual responsibility and in the other because of the brutalizing of sovereignty.

Although many complex factors bear on this situation, a major ingredient is the development of subjective relativism which has tended to destroy overarching values and to make every man's evaluations as valid in theory as any other—inasmuch as there is no way for finite man to grasp final truth. In one way or another the problems of authority can be traced back to this inability of men to agree on common values, goals, and purposes.

How this situation eventuated constitutes a complicated story, but the outlines of the epistemological, subjective relativism that presses in on modern man can be seen taking shape in such men as Descartes, Hume, Kant, Schopenhauer, Hegel, Schleiermacher, Kierkegaard, Nietzsche, and a host of lesser figures. Descartes took a giant step toward subjectivizing all knowledge when he made "I think, therefore I am" his irrefutable starting point. That Descartes failed to establish all knowledge on this basis did not halt the tendency toward the subjectivism and uncertainty of all of man's "truth." By rigorously pursuing this subjective orientation, Descartes by implication made objective truth less acceptable and convincing.

British empiricists such as Locke, later in the same century, made knowledge seem even less secure, especially so far as values are concerned, by depicting the human mind as a more or less empty receptacle that simply receives impressions from the outside. Knowledge and truth are then limited to what the individual can experience. In the eighteenth century, David Hume climaxed this trend with his radical skepticism. He effectively demonstrated that cause and effect in science cannot be proved, that such a mode of thinking is merely the result of custom; that religious miracles are more apt to be the result of duplicity and ignorance than of any divine alteration of nature;

and that the human I, the ego, simply cannot be rationally established as existing. In doing this Hume laid bare the tenuous nature of science, religion, existence, and indeed of all knowledge.

Kant was so disturbed by this trend that he resolved to show the limits of reason in order to make way for faith. In the process he demonstrated the confinement of knowledge to this world of space and time, and, without intending to do so, rendered all knowledge more subjective and relative. Kant maintained that we never know any thing-in-itself. We know only the impressions that we receive from it, these impressions being organized in our minds according to the forms of space and time and the twelve categories, as if the mind were a computer. Knowledge is the computerized product; we do not know the external thing itself. Scientific data is knowledge, not reality; and all knowledge is relative and subjectively conditioned in ways not even considered by Kant.

Kant's *Critique of Pure Reason,* 1781, was seminal for modern man. It limited knowledge to this world of taste, smell, sight, touch, and sound, and at the same time further opened the gates to radical subjective relativism. As Kant did not want to leave the matter there, in the *Critique of Prac-*

24

tical Reason, 1788, he tried to establish a firm basis for ethical action. That basis he discovered in the categorical imperative or moral law which makes it necessary for all men to act in all things as if what they willed were to become universal law. Thus, men are not to murder one another because if murder were universalized as a law the species would be wiped out. Reason, says Kant, demands the moral law; it is necessary for life to make sense. To avoid senselessness, Kant went further and postulated freedom, God, and immortality—not as knowledge—but as necessary to the completion of a rational order. It is rational to assume that to have virtue one must have freedom of choice. It is also rational to assume that virtue should be rewarded and vice punished, but in this world that does not always happen. Therefore, immortality is necessary for virtue and vice to come to their proper ends, and God is necessary to guarantee everything. But the demands of reason do not necessarily coincide with reality. Few people today take Kant's postulates as conclusive, especially if one assumes (as did one of Kant's successors, Schopenhauer) that the world is not orderly.

Schopenhauer argued that ultimate reality, the thing-in-itself, is a giant nonrational will and that everything else is mere idea or illusion, a mirage.

Trees, dogs, rocks, and people exist only as blind objectifications of the will, like bubbles spewed up from some formless glob. In themselves they are nothing. We delude and torture ourselves by thinking that we are something. Salvation lies in the cessation of thought and strife and in the acceptance of the indiscriminate, nonrational, blind will. Existence is sheer illusion.[10]

G. W. F. Hegel, on the other hand, assumed that the thing-in-itself, the essence of reality, is absolute reason in a cosmic process of coming-to-be. Using a model of thesis, antithesis, and synthesis, Hegel traced the process of absolute reason coming to be through universal history. It seemed to reach a pinnacle in Germany and in Hegel himself. Through man the infinite gains self-consciousness.

Schleiermacher was not satisfied with what the rationalists were doing to religion, nor was he satisfied with the institutionalized church. In two epochal works, *Speeches on Religion to Its Cultured Despisers,* 1799, and *The Christian Faith,* 1821–22, Schleiermacher furthered the process of subjective relativism by arguing that religion rests not on rational knowledge nor on past dogmas, but on an immediate consciousness of the all, of our dependence on the absolute. Religious authority

[10] *The World as Will and Idea,* 1818.

then becomes inward feeling! Kierkegaard added his famous contention that subjectivity is truth, all of which leaves man with as many standards or authorities as there are individuals.

With this apparent proliferation of values and truths, Friedrich Nietzsche boldly declared that God is dead, that there is no final standard to which man can appeal, and that everything is permitted. He ruthlessly exposed the old values of love, justice, and mercy as inventions of weak people to disguise their debility. He proclaimed his Superman, who asserts himself and lives by might regardless of what others do. Empirical might he extolled as the governing factor in all affairs, and might has no standard except that which the Superman wishes arbitrarily to enforce.

In many ways Nietzsche is the herald of our twentieth century which, with its totalitarianism and military conflagration, exhibits widespread appeal to force and at the same time a collapse of other commonly accepted values. The two are not unrelated, for man must have society in order to live. If voluntary agreement on common standards and goals becomes impossible, then to avoid an anarchy of sovereign individuals, resort to force would seem to be a necessity.

Yet, there are nihilists who would not agree

even to this. Why have society? With death pressing in upon us, with truth no more than subjective relativism, what is the point of doing anything? Is not all of man's striving, loving, hating, and glorifying a farce? Since no one knows final truth, each person will presumably seek his own inclinations. Since death is the end of everything, why not take what enjoyment is still possible? Indeed nihilism seems to be rampant in our world in the form of insatiable consumption, pollution, and destruction. Why sacrifice? Nothing matters. As Nietzsche and Dostoievsky both noted, nihilism arises when ultimate standards, God, disappear.

To know that nihilism is pervasive in our culture one has only to read Jean-Paul Sartre, Albert Camus, Ernest Hemingway, T. S. Eliot, Edna St. Vincent Millay, Tennessee Williams, Günter Grass, Samuel Beckett, Edward Albee. In our time, epistemological relativism has given way to nihilism in which everything is permitted. Not only do we not agree on overarching values, but we must deal with the possibility that there may be no meaning at all. If there is no meaning, authority becomes senseless, absurd. Yet in our century we have the spectacle of massive totalitarianism. Logically this paradoxical incongruity may be difficult to understand, but it has ample historical precedents, for man seems unable to bear the burden of absolute freedom and autonomy. To escape the specter of anarchy, frustration, and meaninglessness that are inherent in individual autonomy, individuals willingly accept authority.[11] This was part of the secret of Dostoievsky's Grand Inquisitor. Men cannot face the uncertainty of exercising their freedom nor the haunting possibility that everything may be meaningless, so they are willing to sacrifice their freedom for an illusion of security. The Grand Inquisitor assured them that all would be well even though he knew that beyond the grave they would find nothing but death.[12] In *The Flies*, Jean-Paul Sartre pictures the people of Argos in much the same way; they are unable to face freedom; they prefer to feel the sting of the flies, to be directed, to wallow in a "bitchy odor of repentance." Uncertain, scared, they lay their freedom at the feet of Zeus.[13]

Pages from history tend to substantiate these fictional insights. Hitler's totalitarianism was not

---

[11] See "Authority and Freedom: The State and Man," by Hans Buchheim in *Freedom and Authority in the West*, pp. 71 ff.

[12] *The Brothers Karamazov*, pp. 308, 311, 317-18, 321.

[13] See *No Exit and Three Other Plays* (New York: Vintage Books, 1949).

the result of the madness of a few individuals, nor of cunning, trickery, and force, but rather of the choice of a people who sought to escape from the terrible isolation, anxiety, and powerlessness that freedom brings. So writes Erich Fromm in *Escape from Freedom*.[14]

The anarchy and terror of the French Revolution created much the same effect, so that the despotism of Napoleon was a welcome relief. De Maistre (1754–1821) argued that to avoid the pitfalls of skepticism and anarchy men are willing and ought to accept monarchical sovereignty and papal infallibility without asking why.[15] He exalted order above liberty, extolled obedience as the primary political virtue, and considered the executioner the bulwark of social order. Edmund Burke glorified authority in reaction to the excesses of the French Revolution, which he regarded as a violent attempt to repudiate the accumulated achievements of civilization.[16] François de Chateaubriand sought to save men from the perils of reason as manifested in the French situation and guide them back to the folds of authoritarian faith.[17] In view of the wide-

[14] (New York: Rinehart & Co., 1941), pp. 5-6.
[15] *Du Papae*, Bk. 1, chap. 1.
[16] *Reflections on the Revolution in France,* 1790.
[17] *Génie du Christianisme,* 1802.

spread reaction in Roman Catholicism to the modernism which the French Revolution symbolized, one might even regard Pius IX's "Syllabus of Errors," 1864, and Pius X's "Oath Against Modernism," 1910, as climaxes in this trend.

More than a hundred years earlier, during the Puritan Revolution, Thomas Hobbes wrote his *Leviathan*. In it he argued powerfully against the intolerableness of individual autonomy in society. With the monarchy in disarray, with civil war raging, it was as if men had returned to the original state of nature when man was subject to no law but brutal self-interest. In that state every man was autonomous and miserable, for every man was against his neighbor, carrying on a constant warfare, rendering all of life for the so-called free individual "solitary, poor, nasty, brutish, and short." To escape from this warring condition, Hobbes argued, men ought to unite to form a civil society. They should willingly draw up a contract in which they would surrender all their rights to a sovereign who in turn would be strong enough to protect them. For the sake of stability and security Hobbes advocated a return to the rule of monarchy, the Leviathan, whose despotic rule would be better than every man exercising his own freedom or religious groups vying with each other. Individual and group freedom were to Hobbes "worms in the entrails of Leviathan." With relief Englishmen welcomed the restoration of Charles II in 1660.

The insights of these men are not without their blind spots, but each of them points to an apparently central truth about man. He is social as well as individual, and to have society he *must have authority*. Absolute freedom with its overtones of relativism, chaos, and nihilism is not tolerable. Any such situation has to be overridden in order to have society—hence the rise of totalitarianism at a time when agreement on purposes and goals has collapsed. Authority is necessary for human community, but the obedience that undergirds authority must be made freely and responsibly. To have authority in this sense depends on a return to a consensus of values. What symbols, myths, epistemologies, events, or structures will bring this about, or even that it will come about, is not yet evident.

In the context of a massive disenchantment caused by the erosion of values, the issues of authority urgently manifest themselves. Each of the three essays in this book treat an aspect of this overall problem.

Father John L. McKenzie's incisive criticism of the papacy is a case in point. The papacy as an institution arose in response to religious need; it was not just the product of a despotic drive to power. Yet human ambition and pride brought about claims of absolute primacy not only in spiritual, but also in secular affairs. Infallibility has been the functioning principle of the papacy from the early Middle Ages to the present, but this has not been without its critics both within and outside the Roman fold. The Eastern Orthodox churches never acknowledged the supremacy of Rome, and within the Roman Church a clamor arose for representative rule, especially during those periods when worldly interests of the papacy seemed to outweigh anything else and when some of the popes became noted more for their immoralities than their graces. In the fourteenth century France dominated the papacy and moved the papal throne to Avignon, from where the popes ruled from 1309 to 1377, during the "Babylonian Captivity." When this situation was broken, matters only became worse; a schism resulted in which one pope ruled from Avignon and another from Rome. This lasted until 1409 when the Council of Pisa tried unsuccessfully to dethrone the two popes, but was successful in electing a third. During this time conciliarists from all over Europe demanded a truly representative council of the church to take charge. The Council of Constance, 1414–1418, was finally constituted, declared itself the ruling body in the church, and after considerable difficulty got rid of the three reigning popes. However, after the Council of Constance, power gradually gravitated back to the papal office (despite the abortive efforts of the Council of Florence) and by 1460 Pope Pius II was able to condemn anyone who even so much as appealed to a council. The Council of Trent, 1545–1563, which some leaders hoped would move toward conciliar reform, actually strengthened the papacy as the final authority and judge of Scripture and tradition. Papal infallibility followed in 1870, and not until Vatican Council II did a new struggle break out—this time over collegiality and religious freedom. Since then, as Cardinal Bea observed, a thousand horses have run out the barn door. While the dogmas of the Catholic Church have not greatly altered, relativism and skepticism have become marked in both laity and clergy, in line with the doubts about "truth" that have become common in our time. Thousands are no longer willing to obey, and they belligerently protest, yet the papacy insists that its "infallible" pronouncements be heeded. Clergy and laity want a larger voice in decisions that so directly affect them.

The Rev. Albert B. Cleage, Jr., recognizes the ambiguity and cultural aspects of all truth, and boldly declares that his standard of authority is anything that promotes the liberation of Blacks. If something promotes the liberation of Blacks, it is good; if not, it is bad. This forthright declaration underscores the tenuous subjective relativism that eats at the heart of authority. Consequently, not until "ultimates" acceptable to both Whites and Blacks are agreed upon will the authority necessary to curb anarchy, violence, and terror (both incipient and overt) be established. As the Rev. Cleage astutely observes, police power and military power are not enough.

Professor Roger L. Shinn realizes the absence of final authorities and examines the process of how viable agreements can be implemented to represent the desires of the majority without doing violence to the minority, while at the same time incorporating the knowledge of the expert. In the absence of epistemological and moral finalities, some such workable process may be the only recourse left open to man. Whether such a process

35

will be both flexible and stable enough to carry the burden of society and allow for individual freedom will depend on numerous complex factors.

The following three essays probe one of the most profound problems of our time.

AUTHORITY CRISIS
IN ROMAN CATHOLICISM

john l. mckenzie

There are several reasons for choosing to speak on the authority crisis in Roman Catholicism before this audience, which is predominantly Protestant. The first and most obvious reason is that I am better acquainted with this problem of authority than I am with any other. The second is the interest which may be presumed in this ecumenical age in the problems of churches other than one's own. The third is that the authority crisis in the Roman Church, which has traditionally affirmed ecclesiastical authority in a way paralleled in no other Christian church, exhibits both a magnitude and a paradigmatic character all its own. If authority in the Roman Church experiences a crisis, then who is safe from crisis? Or may Protestants feel that the crisis will drive Romanism to a more democratic—and presumably more Protestant—ecclesial polity? To these and to a number of related questions I cannot promise a certain answer, and perhaps not even an educated guess.

The authority in question in the present crisis is understood in Roman Catholicism as operative in two areas: government and teaching. A full explanation of the exercise of authority in Roman Catholicism would leave no time to speak of the crisis; some general knowledge must be presumed. I have adverted to the fact that the Roman understanding and use of authority is unparalleled in other churches; and it may be worth noticing that Protestants have often had an exaggerated idea of the scope of authority in the Roman Church. Both government and teaching are subject to restraints which are usually less apparent than the exercise of authority. The existence of restraints does not alter the theoretical absolutism of authority in the Roman Church, for absolute authority is not by definition an authority which has no restraints. It does mean, I take it, an authority which is not

38

restrained constitutionally by the will of the governed.

It is no doubt an element of the crisis that Catholics attempt to preserve the language of the past even if they believe that the institutions of the past are dissolving, or even if they are taking action toward the dissolution of the institutions. Some contemporary discussions give the impression of speech with a forked tongue. The impression is not entirely inaccurate. Many—and I include myself—have no massive scheme of new structures with which we intend to replace the old. Until we have devised new structures, we have no language in which to discuss structure except the language of the old. Still others, whom I have to classify as less moderate, seem to be more interested in dispossessing the existing authorities of their power than they are in creating new structures of power. I would not yet say that this extreme view is representative, but it is certainly an element of the crisis which causes a peculiar anxiety as long as it retains the possibility of growth.

The crisis in government is a clerical crisis rather than an ecclesiastical crisis up to this point. That the crisis has not had a wider impact is not due to any theoretical renunciation of power over the laity, but simply to the fact that the Roman Church does not attempt to exercise over the laity the kind of power it exercises over the clergy. If one seeks the root of the crisis, one finds it, in spite of the risk of oversimplification, in a refusal to accept absolute power restrained only by the prudence, wisdom, and charity of those who bear it. This refusal has become explicit in certain specific areas, and by surveying them we shall have surveyed the crisis in government. These areas are the relations of the pope with the bishops, of the Roman curia with bishops and clergy, and of bishops and other religious superiors with priests and members of religious orders.

The relations of the pope with the bishops are now summed up in the problem of collegiality. Theologians know that solid theological work on this problem has not been done. The Roman Church has stated the power of the pope much more clearly than it has stated the power of the bishops. It is troubled by the theoretical problem of overlapping jurisdictions, and the problem has become practical as well as theoretical in recent years. That it did not become practical sooner was due to the readiness of the body of bishops to accept the Roman understanding of a bishop as a vicar of the Roman pontiff. This is not a sound theological understanding of the episcopacy; and a sound understanding, when it is developed, will be more subtle than the theory of emperor and satraps, which is more or less what the Roman practice has presupposed. When practice discords with theory as widely as the Roman practice does, a crisis is inevitable. Nor is this the kind of crisis which can be postponed to a time when there is no feeling on the question. The time when the use of authority can be discussed without feeling never comes. Let there be no misunderstanding; the intention of many bishops is to restrain the papal government by the expression of the will of the bishops. These restraints are meant to be real, not mere restraints of courtesy. The actual power of the papacy in collegiality will be diminished.

I have separated the Roman curia as a distinct crisis area from the papacy, although this separation has some difficult implications. Let it be said that the Roman Catholic Church cannot conceive itself without the papacy. It has no trouble at all conceiving itself without the Roman curia. The Roman curia is the vast bureaucracy through which, in the words of the code of canon law, the Roman pontiff is accustomed to transact the business of the universal church. This bureaucracy has been centuries growing; and criticisms of its personnel and its operations were voiced before the reformers (of the sixteenth century). It verifies the classical remark about the Bourbons; it has learned nothing and forgotten nothing. It is predominantly Italian in its personnel. As obvious to any observer, the Roman curia fattens itself to the degree to which the absolute power of the papacy is acknowledged in the Roman Church. It has been charged with corruption for most of the last six hundred years; but it is one of the few institutions in the world which maintains its freedom to reform itself. As one might expect, this means it has never been reformed. Discontent with the papacy is not the same thing as discontent with the Roman curia; but since the papacy has no operations which are not the operations of the Roman curia, the line sometimes is too fine to be seen. The proved incompetence and dishonesty of the Roman curia are enough to provoke a crisis in any society which is not totally insensitive. It is my personal opinion that the Roman Catholic crisis of authority is radicated in the Roman curia. Theoretically the curia is the staff of the pope, entirely selected by his personal appointment. In reality it is a self-perpetuating governing clique which outlives any pope as the State Department outlives any president. The late John XXIII is credited with saying that it was the sack in which he was tied up.

42

Whether he actually said this or not, the statement described the relations of the pope with the curia accurately.

Since the Roman curia is not a constitutive element of the Roman Church, it is a self-evident theological truth that the pope could annihilate it, reform it, replace it with another structure at any time he wishes. The failure of the popes to take action in an area where they have complete freedom to act aggravates the crisis. Dissatisfaction with the Roman curia is deep and widespread among bishops and clergy, and it is spreading to the laity. If the popes are unable to act, and not merely unwilling, then the crisis is even more acute. The real target of the episcopal synod is the Roman curia, not the Roman pontiff. It is quite true that the Roman pontiff without the Roman curia might become King Log, but the Roman curia has become so impossible that many seem to feel the risk is worth taking.

Collegiality in a larger and not entirely accurate sense is also sought on the level of dioceses and religious communities, those groups of professional religious persons who carry on the daily work of the Roman Catholic Church. Collegiality in these groups is not understood in the sense that a bishop or a religious superior becomes a primate among his

43

colleagues. What is meant is that the traditional total submission in religious bodies, often praised as "blind obedience," should be replaced by something called a shared decision or decision with a broader base of consent. The traditional understanding and practice of obedience made it unnecessary or even inexpedient for religious superiors to consult their subjects about anything; I have read and heard superiors of another generation say that it is imprudent for a superior to give reasons for his decisions because the reasons might furnish an occasion for criticism. It was assumed that the subject, by the choice of his state of life, had renounced any personal ideas, ambitions, or feelings which could affect the decisions of his superior; and it was thought only such total submission gave the religious superior the freedom which he needed in government.

This understanding and practice has never been realistic, and never free from problems; wits have described the system as absolutism tempered by rebellion. It worked because it was rarely administered according to the theory. It is not merely its unrealism which creates the crisis, it is the growing conviction that this kind of obedience is degrading to the human person. It is also an awareness of the tremendous potential of abuse which this obedience has if command falls into unworthy hands. Many priests and religious people wonder whether anyone has the gifts of mind, heart, and grace to administer such a despotism in a worthy manner. The crisis of authority at this level reveals itself in a new and disturbing manner in a sudden jump in the numbers of those who leave the professional religious vocation and a sudden shrinking in the number of those who enter the vocation. The gravity of the crisis is emphasized up to this time by the failure of any prelate to state clearly and publicly that there is anything wrong with the system of government which so many people are refusing to accept.

Whether the press is a contributing factor to the crisis is disputed. It seems safer to say that the press reports the crisis rather than creates it, in spite of the alarm and indignation expressed by many Catholics who do not believe that dirty linen should be washed in public. Whether the alleged denial of certain basic human freedoms or offenses against basic human decency should be likened to soiled linen I am not prepared to say. The government of the Roman Catholic Church entered the twentieth century with a complete set of medieval and Renaissance traditions of administration. Absolute government works best when its processes are secret. As long as Catholics believed that absolutism was given to the Catholic Church by the institution of Jesus Christ, they were ready to swallow some unwholesome features in order to preserve the system. As a whole, Catholics no longer believe that the Catholic Church must govern absolutely to observe the mandate of Jesus Christ. The press has certainly contributed to this change of attitude, and to this extent it can be said to contribute to the crisis; but it is necessary to ask what its contribution has been.

The Vatican Council II was the first major assembly in the history of Catholicism to be fully reported in the contemporary press, and we easily remember how much opposition there was to the publication of its deliberations. An entirely unintended by-product, I am sure, was the discovery by the press that the church can be news. Closer journalistic observation of the Roman Catholic Church rendered public a certain amount of information which had always been known by the professional religious persons in the Catholic Church; they had never published this information partly because of a kind of corporate loyalty, but also because they thought people in general were simply not interested. It has turned out instead that people have found the insensitive autocracy of many Roman Catholic prelates to be intolerably scandalous. They can hardly believe that a transaction like the dealings of Cardinal McIntyre[1] with the Sisters of the Immacuate Heart of Mary was a simple routine procedure to his Eminence, to the Holy See, and to a large but undetermined number of bishops. They find it equally scandalous that those bishops who disapprove have no way of expressing their disapproval. If this is routine in the government of the Roman Catholic Church, they think, then the routine operations of the Roman Catholic Church may be as a whole indefensible and unsupportable. They would not think so if this were not reported in the press, but the press did not create the situation.

We turn to the crisis of the teaching authority, which has come to full bloom in less than a year. That it could mature so quickly after the publication of the encyclical *Humanae Vitae*[2] shows clearly that the materials of the crisis were already there and needed only an occasion to burst into

[1] James F. McIntyre, cardinal since 1953, Los Angeles. —EDITOR'S NOTE.

[2] July 29, 1968. The encyclical branded as illicit every effort to curb procreation in the conjugal act. Many protests followed. For a discussion of the controversy caused in the Roman Catholic Church by this encyclical see *Dissent in and for the Church: Theologians and Humanae Vitae* (New York: Sheed & Ward, 1969).—EDITOR'S NOTE.

flames. It is my personal conjecture, not previously presented to the public, that the Holy See neither sought nor expected a crisis of the teaching authority. I believe it was the conviction of the Roman curia that the teaching authority of the papacy would have been hopelessly compromised if the pope had said anything which even failed to repeat what his predecessors had said, for they thought that the image of an infallible authority had to be preserved at any cost. The settlement of a particular moral problem, or the peace of conscience of Catholics, or the moral impossibilities which might fall upon married people were all less important than preserving the image of the pope as God's infallible spokesman. The duty of the papacy was first of all to preserve its own image. The Roman curia, I believe, which has its own brand of realism, expected that the encyclical would be devoutly received, duly praised, and totally ignored. Its authors knew that it was an impossible moral guide, and expected Catholics to recognize its purpose and its meaning.

I am fully aware that this conjectural interpretation presumes an appalling cynicism in the supreme government of the Roman Catholic Church. Were this the first instance of such cynicism in the history of the papacy, I would suppress it. What is known about the deliberation which preceded the encyclical really leaves no room for any other interpretation. The Roman curia was not so unrealistic that it thought it could conceal the fact that the majority of Catholic learning, represented by a group which, we can be sure, was not selected for its radicalism, was opposed to the thesis of the encyclical. One must suppose that even curial theologians could recognize where the evidence was. One has heard some of them quoted as saying that papal infallibility is hopelessly compromised by any other action than the action the pope took, whatever be the merits of the case. They turned the moral question into an ecclesiological question, and by doing so they rendered the moral problem insoluble.

The failure of the Catholic body to go along with this cynical purpose—which I for one expected the Catholic body to do—compelled the papacy to reassert its teaching authority in even stronger terms. The papacy was willing to have its teaching ignored—this was not new; it was unwilling and will remain unwilling to have its teaching authority challenged. Protestants may not generally know that Roman Catholic theology has long provided a position for those who feel in conscience that they cannot accept a pontifical doctrine which is not proposed in the manner which theologians call "solemn." Vatican spokesmen have often said that the encyclical is not solemn. But the theological hypothesis always presupposed that those who demurred would be few in number; it was not prepared for a massive rejection of a pontifical doctrine, a massive rejection to which even some episcopal conferences seemed sympathetic. In one diocese, Washington, a notable number of priests were suspended until submission, which has not yet happened. In other dioceses priest-teachers were removed from teaching. In most of the world nothing at all happened to publicly dissenting priests. The confusion after the encyclical is even worse than it was before. The teaching authority of the Roman Catholic Church is experiencing its most serious crisis since the Reformation, but with some notable differences; those who dissent from the teaching authority are neither rejecting the authority of nor departing from the Roman Catholic communion.

It seems no more than fair to say that the pope is responsible for this crisis; and I speak of the pope as an institution, not as a person. The Vatican reveals neither its deliberations nor the persons involved in them nor the processes employed. This seems a fair assessment of responsibility because it is a fair judgment that the encyclical imposed an extremely rigorous moral restraint without adducing equally rigorous evidence for the obligation. This can only be called an abuse of authority; and one realizes rather suddenly that while Catholics have been ready to admit that the governing authority of the Catholic Church is subject to abuse, they have been reluctant to admit that the teaching authority can also be abused. Most Catholics are not widely informed on theology and church history; if they were, they would not be so anxious to maintain some vestiges of the divine attributes in the papacy. I suspect that Paul VI has deprived the teaching authority of the Catholic Church of prestige which it will take at least two hundred years to recover.

This pessimism may have to be moderated by the fact that the Second Vatican Council produced a collection of documents which have been more respectfully and favorably received both within and outside the Roman Catholic Church than any utterance the church has ever made. I am reminded of a conversation with the late Dean Samuel Miller, an observer of the Council, in which he opined that we Catholics were harsh and unfair to such gracious gentlemen as Cardinal Ottaviani. The same Dean Miller, when the document on religious freedom was postponed, was quoted in the press

as saying that he had seen the naked face of
Vatican power on the floor of Saint Peter's that day.
What had happened to the gracious gentlemen?
Dean Miller had recognized what we Catholics
have long known. Similarly, I fear that others like
Dean Miller will regard the Second Vatican Coun-
cil as ecumenical window dressing and *Humanae
Vitae* as the naked face of the real Vatican. Neither
is a true understanding. The problem and the
crisis of the Roman Catholic teaching authority is
that it can produce both the acts of the Second
Vatican Council and the encyclical *Humanae
Vitae*.

Appeals to collegiality sometimes suggest that
had the pope consulted the synod of bishops,
Humanae Vitae would not have appeared. There
is no way of speculating what would have happened. It is true that the synod has now recom-
mended that no similar statements be issued without consulting the body of bishops; this hardly
looks like a recommendation of *Humanae Vitae*.
But it leads us to ask whether the Roman Church
recognizes its crisis of authority and whether it is
taking any action. I believe that the answer to both
questions is affirmative, but this does not resolve
the crisis.

Collegiality is not the one antidote for the Roman

Catholic problems of authority, certainly not if it is understood as referring only to the relations of the papacy with the bishops. A papacy identified with the existing Roman curia simply cannot enter into collegial relations with the bishops, and in particular because the curia retains a monopoly on episcopal appointments. The theoretical dispute between pontifical appointment and popular election of bishops could go on without resolution to the Second Coming; and it would never touch the manifest fact that the Roman curia has proved beyond doubt its incapacity to find able and worthy bishops in sufficient numbers. It is not really a question of whether election is a better way, but simply a fact that it is the only alternative to the present intolerable way.

Decentralization is a word often heard in the Roman Church in recent years; as yet it designates nothing in the world of reality. Linked with decentralization is internationalization of the Roman curia. For a moment let us forget the bland amenities and recognize that when Catholics talk about the internationalization of the curia they really mean that they wish to release the church from Italian control. This does not mean that they wish to see the control pass into the hands of some other national group. There is a thing in Catholi-

cism called *Romanita*. This means acceptance not of
Roman Catholic doctrine and liturgy, but of a
clerical-cultural pattern which is Roman, not
Italian, for *Romanita* is disliked in Florence and
Milan too. It appears in men of other countries
who reside long in Rome, and who manifest some
desire to advance in the Roman Catholic clerical
cursus honorum [course of honors]. Such men
become more Roman than the Romans; and since
wit has not died in Italy, such overenthusiastic
adopted Italians are often laughed at by the native
Italians. But they are used because of their un-
wavering fidelity to the ideals of *Romanita*. As long
as *Romanita* endures, talk about internationalization
of the curia is idle. Action required here is of such
magnitude and such difficulty that it sometimes
looks like an effort to abolish the papacy itself.

I have adverted to one important difference
between the crisis of the Roman Church in the
sixteenth century and its present crisis. This is the
unwillingness of Catholics to renounce their mem-
bership, and in particular to establish other
churches. The "underground" church has come into
existence; these groups are discontented and dis-
affected, but they are not dissident. They intend
to remain Roman Catholic, and they nearly defy
the official church to find a way to expel them

There has long been a tacit acceptance of the identification of the church with the hierarchy and the clergy. As closely as one can tell, a large number of Catholics no longer accept this identification. The effects of this change of attitude upon church authority may be too far-reaching to analyze at present. To return to one of my original questions, everything points to a change in the direction of a more democratic—and therefore more Protestant?—use of authority in the Roman Catholic Church. If the discontented will not depart and refuse to be expelled, they will sooner or later be heard. In previous crises the Roman authority could preserve itself by lopping off the troublemakers.

E. H. Chamberlin has recently published a book entitled *The Bad Popes.*[3] In my own review of this book I came to the depressing conclusion that no single person or institution has been a greater obstacle to faith in Roman Catholic Christianity than the papacy, and it is depressing because the papacy can neither be abolished nor replaced. I will now add that the papacy can be relativized, if that is the correct word to describe the change of an absolute power; and the relativizing of the papacy should extend to the episcopacy. The

[3] (New York: Dial Press, 1969).

Roman Church will not resolve its crisis by exchanging one absolutism for another. I will add also that the history of the papacy can, by a somewhat distorted synthesis, be viewed as a series of waves in each of which the papacy tends to move toward a supremacy of power which escapes it at the moment of crisis. Because the papacy does not reform itself, it is forced to await the reforming action of history. But the reforming action of history is not really reforming; the purifying flame of catastrophe is a pleasant metaphor for senseless destruction. The pride and pomp of Boniface VIII suffered a cruel blow at Anagni,[4] and the foolish secular politics of Clement VII collapsed in the sack of Rome.[5] In more recent times the vigorous

[4] Pope Boniface VIII, 1294–1303, after claiming supreme authority over secular and spiritual affairs in his famous *Unam Sanctam* of 1302, was attacked and taken prisoner at Anagni by the military forces of King Philip IV of France. Pope Boniface died a month later. Pope Benedict XI, 1303–1304, his successor, died mysteriously after issuing a bull against the outrage at Anagni. After eleven months had passed, Clement V, 1305-1313, was elected pope. He moved the papacy to Avignon, France, thus beginning the "Babylonian Captivity" of the papacy which lasted until 1377. —EDITOR'S NOTE.

[5] Pope Clement VII, 1523–1534, tried to steer a path between the rival aims of Francis I of France and Emperor Charles V. His irresolute policies resulted in the sack of Rome by the imperial forces of Charles V in 1527.—EDITOR'S NOTE.

reactionary policies of Pius IX [6] trapped him in the Vatican Palace and alienated him from his own people. Such "reformations" can be neither planned nor predicted, nor can they even be desired. Worse than that, they do not always reform.

The simple fact of the moment is that the power and prestige of the papacy and the Roman Catholic hierarchy have been seriously weakened. The clergy and laity do not give them that childlike and docile submission which they have learned to expect, and will not give it again during the lifetime of anyone now living. I would not prognosticate the collapse of the whole structure; one of the most futile games theologians play is forecasting the end of Roman Catholicism. At the minimum one can expect the papacy and the hierarchy to make the minimum concessions they must make to remain in business—that is, they will yield what power they must in order not to lose it all. This would be political bargaining of the most gross worldly type, but the Roman curia has proved that

[6] Pope Pius IX, 1846–1878, promulgated the "Immaculate Conception of the Blessed Virgin Mary," 1854, and the "Syllabus of Errors," 1864, and engineered the statement on papal infallibility at Vatican Council I, 1870. Unable to accept the Law of Guarantees of the newly formed Kingdom of Italy, Pius retreated to his Vatican Palace and referred to himself as the "prisoner of the Vatican."—EDITOR'S NOTE.

it is not above this type of bargaining. At the other extreme would be a charismatic outpouring of the Spirit which would diffuse through the Roman Catholic body the idea that authority is service in love. Between these two extremes is a wide spectrum of possibilities, and I see no way at the moment of defining the possibilities more closely.

A BLACK MAN'S
VIEW OF AUTHORITY
albert b. cleage, jr.

The question of authority is a complex one. Any individual's approach depends upon his definition of many things. We could go through the empty motions of an academic discussion, but I would prefer to begin by giving an indication of where I stand and thereby prepare you to evaluate my conclusions.

I believe that there are, essentially, two Americas—a White America and a Black America. There are two Christian churches, a White church and a Black church. We are in the midst of a gigantic social upheaval, and the continuation of American society as it now exists is an impossibility. We are in the midst of change. I am speaking as a Black man, and I am very anxious that change proceed as rapidly as possible, and that the society that now exists be radically altered as quickly and as completely as possible. So I approach the problem of authority differently than I would if I considered myself a part of this society and accepted the continuation of existing authority as basic to its continued existence. I accept one fundamental authority: the Black liberation struggle as it is shaped by the Black experience. By the yardstick of that struggle and that experience all things must be judged and evaluated, maintained or discarded.

A determinative aspect of the Black experience in the Western world is the continuing Black liberation struggle. Even the dream of integration constituted a phase of that struggle by which all things must be judged. If it supports the liberation struggle of Black people, then it is good. If it is in opposition to the liberation struggle of Black people, then it is bad. If it supports the liberation struggle of Black people, then it is moral. If it opposes the liberation struggle of Black people, then it is immoral. If it supports the liberation struggle of Black people, then it is the will of God. If it opposes the liberation struggle of Black people, then it is in opposition to the will of God; it is the action of Satan. And so with this simplistic key to the mysteries of life I have little difficulty in evaluating either events or institutions.

We cannot really discuss authority without considering power, because in the final analysis, authority depends upon power for its existence. The power or sanction by which authority is maintained may be more apparent than real, as is true with the police power of a state or with the god-power of an ecclesiastical institution. The authority of a state cannot be maintained by police power alone for the simple reason that no state has sufficient police power. This becomes increasingly obvious as a society in the midst of chaos and conflict tries to maintain itself. Remember the Detroit rebellion of 1967 (which you may still call a riot) and the rebellions which swept the country in '65, '66 and '67. If in any five or six cities, rebellions comparable to the rebellion in Detroit had broken out, it would have been utterly impossible for the police power of America to have maintained authority of the state without calling home front-line troops from Vietnam, and whether or not they could have been gotten back in time is questionable.

During the Detroit Freedom March in 1963,

approximately 200,000 Black people walked down Woodward Avenue with Dr. Martin Luther King, and I will never forget the pathetic sight of police officers assigned to keep order and the policemen on motorcycles who were expected to keep the marchers in an orderly procession. Their frightened faces as they tried to stay out of the way revealed their knowledge that this crowd of 200,000 Black people could have walked them into the asphalt of the street without even striking a blow. The preponderance of sheer people power reduced to absurdity the thought that a few thousand police officers could keep order. And so I say the authority of the state cannot be maintained by police power alone. The citizens of a state must be programmed to believe that the authority of the state ought to be accepted, because it is right; and that the power of the state is invincible, even though it is not.

So actually the power of the state is mythological. The state can exist only so long as the people permit it to exist. This has been stated in many ways with the whole compact theory of society. The Declaration of Independence declares that governments exist by the consent of the governed. This is true, and yet, the police power of a state is important, because during ordinary times most of the people in a state believe in the rightness of the things the police protect and are prepared to accept the authority of the state. They believe that police power ought to be used when necessary to maintain the state against attacks by disgruntled minorities who would subvert the rights of the majority.

The authority of an ecclesiastical institution is founded upon its mythological godpower, and this can be most embarrassing when it cannot produce its godpower in time of crisis. When a society needs the godpower for which it has paid in the building of churches, the payment of salaries, and the training of experts in the art of godpower manipulation, ecclesiastical institutions are expected to make immediate delivery. And people in a society which is in the process of change find their churches nonrelevant and meaningless when they cannot do the thing for which they were created. The church must maintain the stability of the social order, put down the unwashed legions who declare the society evil and unjust, and thwart all attacks upon the status quo. The authority of any ecclesiastical institution rests upon its ability to program its followers to believe that it actually has the godpower to do these things. Services of worship are designed to keep people conscious of this power which the church supposedly has available for use. Here again we can see the mythological nature of the power upon which authority is presumed to rest.

During a period of social upheaval and general insecurity, people begin to question the godpower of the church because of its obvious inability to alter the course of events. Gallup polls will indicate that most people feel that the church is no longer a satisfactory institution and that the church has failed. And so people in many ways vote against ecclesiastical institutions: by not attending services regularly, by not contributing, by being generally hostile and noncooperative to indicate their general displeasure. This is both reasonable and justifiable because the church, like all social institutions, exists to help maintain the status quo. It is a power institution, and its function is essential to maintain the stability of society by warding off threatening evil spirits which might tend to corrupt sinful men by making them dissatisfied with the existing social order. Its authority is the power of God and the earthly power establishment of which it is a part. People expect it to do the things for which it was created. When it cannot do these things, people are dissatisfied.

This is true in any situation in which authority must be maintained by actual power. In inner-city high schools across the country, the authority of school administrators has been destroyed. School authorities do not have the power to maintain authority. And so an extra-legal student authority has come into being which maintains de facto control of the schools. On many college campuses the administration has been challenged, and large numbers of students have supported the challenge. College administrators have lacked the power to maintain authority. They have been forced to turn to either the city police or the state police for the power to maintain authority. This public admission of their inability to maintain authority without outside power has forced a totally new readjustment of the relationship of college administrator and student body on the American college campus. A new concept of authority is emerging. In short, authority depends upon power for its existence, but wielders of authority rarely possess more than the illusion of power, and depend in large measure upon passive acceptance. In fact, much of the talk about authority deals with illusion rather than with reality. A biblical scholar will maintain in all seriousness that the "authority of the Old Testament" is much less than the "authority of the New Testament," because much of the Old Testament does not measure up to the high ethical and spiritual standard revealed by Jesus in the

New Testament. To prove this point, he will completely misinterpret the revolutionary message of Jesus in the New Testament and completely overlook the fact that the actual teachings of Jesus are but an extension of the Old Testament. He is not dealing with "authority," but with an ecclesiastical illusion which is necessary to enable the church to serve its social function in the world.

A group, any group, of any color, and in any geographic part of the world, comes together only upon the basis of power and self-interest. A mob of individuals coalesces because self-interest dictates that only through coming together can they increase their individual power. For no other reason will individuals subordinate their desire for status and recognition and their individualistic seeking after power. The individual coalesces with a group because through the group he can satisfy his individual lust for power by seeing the group as an extension of himself and his self-interest.

A mob becomes a group (or a nation) when it recognizes the simple fact that by necessity it must accept the authority of leaders and institutions created to serve its power interests. Each individual gives up something of his individualistic lust for power in order that he can merge with a group and share a larger vision of power with a far

greater possibility of success. He accepts the necessity for the authority of leaders and institutions,
which he helps create to serve his power interests,
by serving the power interests of the group of
which he is a part. Once established, however,
institutions seem to take on a kind of independent
existence. Even though we forget the circumstances
out of which they came into being, they are
necessary to the power of the group, and automatic
mechanisms exist to protect these power institutions; and when any of them are threatened, the
individuals who make up the group experience a
spontaneous emotional reaction of discomfort, of
being personally threatened. The group reacts with
protective hostility to anything which threatens
its power institutions, and as an individual you
will react with a hostility which you cannot explain
on a personal basis when the institutions which
are an extension of your power hunger are
threatened by outside forces.

Just as a group comes together, sets up institutions, delegates and accepts authority, those who are
excluded from power eventually coalesce in order
to attack the power establishment. They seek to
destroy the authority of the power establishment
and to structure the transference of power to
themselves. This attack can be either within the

existing rules, as is the case with the Black revolution (attacking within the rules established by the dominant White power group), or within a completely new framework established by the creation of a completely new set of rules as is true with a Communist type revolution. Eventually, as the basis of its attack, every revolution must repudiate the authority of the rules established by the dominant power group.

Today's repressive measures are the typical reaction of any society as it begins to collapse under attack. Repression can be seen in the increase of police brutality across the country, in the shooting down of Black Panthers in Northern urban ghettos, and in the general increase of repression and brutality in schools and universities across the land. The general repression of all kinds of dissent in America reflects the general insecurity which has resulted from a multiple attack upon the White power institutions of the Western world. There had to be this kind of repression, there had to be this kind of hostile emotional reaction. The White group was under attack. Its institutions had to be protected. The silent majority of White Americans suddenly began to feel hostile because they realized that they were being attacked upon every front by Black people who were demanding a restructuring of society and by young people who were questioning all of the values upon which the power of their group depends. Feeling themselves attacked from every side, they moved to fortify and protect the institutions which are basic to the preservation of the power and authority of White America.

It is not an accidental thing that Nixon is in the White House at this time, that Middle America is front-page news at this time, that repression is growing at this time, and that the so-called liberal White establishment has begun to feel that it must stop this polarization which is exposing its failure to absorb conflict. And so all across the country the liberal establishment is calling for peace and integration—the anti-defamation leagues, the urban coalitions, the liberal wings of the Protestant denominations which have no power but represent the human relations front of the churches which cannot act on a policy-making level, but serve as a buffer between those who are alienated and those who are in power. These groups are coming together to issue joint statements. The repressive measures are as necessary for the preservation of White power as the joint liberal statements are futile. Some naïve Christians dare to wonder why there can still be reactionaries and

conservatives in the churches after all the years
of preaching. After all the years of preaching!
That's what the churches are for! That is the
purpose of the churches! We can only wonder that
for so many years the authority of the power
establishment was so secure that it was unnecessary
for the churches to voice the conservatism which
is essential to protect the overall institutionalization
of White supremacy. But now authority is being
challenged upon every hand, and the challenging
of authority in the White man's world challenges
his institutions and challenges White supremacy.

The Black man is engaged in a revolution to
restructure American society; and so we—as Black
people—have a very clear-cut position, just as,
increasingly, the Middle American has a very
clear-cut position. Nixon's silent majority insists
that his White churches either defend White
American institutions, or go out of existence. No
White minister in America will for very long be
permitted to preach liberalism, that is to equivocate
as to the authority of existing White institutions.
He will either defend the White power establishment, or he will be driven out of the church, because the church is too important an institution
to be left in the hands of irresponsible White
liberals who had their chance and failed to keep

the peace. Middle America will take control of the church, as it has taken control of the government, and as it will take control of all other White institutions in America. So the Black-White polarization will gradually become complete.

Black people in America have been programmed for inferiority—deliberately, consistently, exquisitely. The White man's declaration of Black inferiority is basic to all of American life. There is no institution in America, no aspect of American life that does not basically reflect the declared inferiority of all Black people. Not poor Black people, not ignorant Black people, not uncouth Black people, but *all* Black people have been declared inferior. This declaration of Black inferiority is the basic foundation upon which American history has been built. From the time Black people were brought to these shores as slaves, the declaration of Black inferiority was the framework within which the Black man was forced to build his existence. In the slave ship, on the slaveblock, on the plantation, fleeing from the lynch mob, fleeing North into slum ghettos, the Black man was not only "declared" inferior but everything possible was done to make that "declaration" a statement of fact. The Black man could accept this declaration of inferiority or he could reject it, and for the early part of his existence in America the Black man did accept the White man's declaration of Black inferiority. As a slave, systematically separated from people who spoke his language, living in a country about which he knew nothing, not even the simple geography necessary to attempt escape, he was forced to accept the authority of the White slave master to define his person and the conditions of his existence.

The Black man had no alternative to an acceptance of the White man's declaration of his inferiority. His freedom had been taken from him; his culture had been taken from him; his history had been taken from him; his language had been taken from him; his dignity had been taken from him; he had nothing left but his physical being and the will to survive. The Black man learned to live with this declaration of Black inferiority, and self-hate became a basic characteristic of the Black man's life in America. As John O. Killens has stated, the White men brought Black men to America and made Niggers out of them.[1]

[1] John O. Killens is the author of three recent books: *Black Man's Burden* (New York: Pocket Books, 1969), *'sippi* (New York: Trident Press, 1967), and *And Then We Heard the Thunder* (New York: Alfred A. Knopf, 1963). —EDITOR'S NOTE.

Integration is the name given to the Black man's slave philosophy of self-hate. The dream of intergration is the Black man's response to the White man's declaration of Black inferiority. The dream of ultimate escape from Blackness has motivated Black people from the days of slavery through the brutal period of reconstruction down to the present. "Integration Now" was the heroic battle cry of Dr. Martin Luther King. "We Shall Overcome" our separation was the anguished cry of the Black man's faith that escape from Blackness was possible. The dream of integration is the Black man's acceptance of the White man's declaration of his inferiority and is a mechanism which perpetuates his enslavement.

This is not easy for White people to understand. For the White oppressor who has declared Black people inferior to say, "I believe in integration" is one thing. But for a Black man—after all of the suffering, the oppression, the brutality, and the inhumanity which he has suffered at the hands of White people—to say, "I believe in the possibility of integration," "I dream of integration," "I work for integration," or "I would accept integration," is obviously a sign of insanity. No Black man in his right mind, in a healthy, normal state of mind, could possibly dream of integration with his enemy.

73

And so the dream of integration which has motivated Black people has been the mechanism by
which our enslavement has been perpetuated. To
dream of integration, a Black man must believe in
the goodness of White people; he must believe
that for some reason what is being done to him
is his own fault, and that he must work to measure
up to White people. Self-hatred is the inevitable
corollary of the dream of integration. "Obviously
there is something wrong with me," the Black man
reasons, "because the White man is superior; he
has everything, he is good, and if he won't accept
me, there has got to be something wrong with
me." For the Black integrationist, self-hate is
inescapable.

The Black man's final fantasy is to believe that
the White man will accept him as an individual
of superior merit, even if he won't accept other
Black people. This means that Black people in the
final analysis are reduced to an individualistic
struggle against each other. Not only do Black
people then in terms of this overall declaration of
Black inferiority hate themselves, but they hate all
other Black people on the simple theory that if it
weren't for all of these other obnoxious Black
people, White people would not hate *me*. The

Black man then begins to hate everything about his community, everything about his culture, everything about his imitation institutions which he has patterned after White institutions, believing that all of these things are inferior because he is inferior. For the Black man to permit the White man to define his being as well as his condition by a declaration of Black inferiority which he accepts is to accept a Black world of self-hatred from which there is no possible escape. The dream of integration then becomes the mechanism of his continuing enslavement.

Everything in the Black community is contaminated by the Black man's efforts to identify with the enemy world of the oppressor. The Black church inherited its God, its Jesus, and its interpretation of the Bible from the White man, the White master. Obviously, the White master was not concerned about giving Black people a revolutionary religion which could liberate them. Naturally, the kind of religion which met the needs of the White master could not possibly meet the needs of the Black slave.

The religion which the master gave to his slave was designed for pacification and to support the authority of White supremacy. He said, "Now, this is a picture of God. This is a picture of Jesus. They are both White as you can plainly see. Here are biblical characters. They're all White. But they love you in spite of your evil Blackness, and they're going to do something for you in the great beyond! You have to live such a life here on earth that after death when you cross over Jordan, there will be a reward for you. Sometimes you think that all the suffering that you are doing down here is passing unnoticed by God, but it's not! God is watching everything, every minute of every day. And for every bit of suffering you have down here God puts all that down! And eventually, on the other side of the Jordan, there will be a reward for you: Milk and honey and golden streets!" So Black people had only to accept the authority of the White world to inherit a glorious reward in heaven.

Black people live in a world in which there is no possibility for dignity or decency of life here on earth. Life is only a testing and a preparation for death and some mystical existence that follows death. It is a beautiful myth, an application of the pagan distortion which the Apostle Paul, following his conversion on the Damascus Road, took to the White Gentile world in the name of Jesus. His fanciful interpretation had almost nothing to do with anything that Jesus ever said or did. Paul assured the authority of the White power establishment. No actual power was needed to perpetuate the Black man's enslavement. Everything that could be done to liberate the Black man had already been accomplished on Calvary two thousand years ago. The Black man needed to do nothing himself except accept his lot and be washed in the blood of the Lamb and be made white like snow (in preparation for the life to come).

So then, if you are Black, you can be poverty stricken, you can be brutalized, and you can still be saved. Your children can be discriminated against and denied a decent education, and you can still be saved. You can live in a neighborhood from which all of the decencies of life have been taken, and you're still saved. It was this kind of primitive Christianity which Black slaves received from their White slave masters. And for many years even this helped Black people survive in situations in which there were few real possibilities to escape from total powerlessness here on earth. The dream that in some mysterious afterlife things would be different at least helped to maintain sanity. Suffering Black people brought to a mystical escapist religion the emotional fervor and "soul" necessary to make it vital and beautiful. We had been programmed for inferiority, and the Black church as an institution contributed to this process. The authority of the Black church was the authority of the White man, of the White slave master, and of the White church with its White God and White Jesus. As Black people we tried to do the things that they said were right because we accepted the White man's definitions along with his power.

This was also true of all other institutions in the Black community. A Black businessman with a little store didn't work too hard in his little store because he wanted to be a part of the great economic thing that the White man had. He wanted to become a part of the White establishment. Black colleges and universities were established as control mechanisms for Black people. White Christians put money into Fisk, Talledega, Atlanta, and other Black schools to teach Black people how to act like White people and to despise everything Black. These so-called Black institutions are still controlled by White people and exist to serve the interests of White people. Why else would they ignore the history and culture of Black people and teach that Black music is inferior, Black art is inferior, Black poetry is inferior, Black literature is inferior, and the totality of the Black experience is something of which Black people should be ashamed and from which they should seek speedy deliverance through education.

So you come to a Black university, really a Negro university. When Black young people enter a Black or rather "Negro" college, kindly well-intentioned White people and brainwashed Black people teach them how to act like White people and take on the refinements of White civilization. This is what a Black college is supposed to do, and this is the process by which the White power establishment perpetuates its authority. This is the kind of structure that White people contribute to even though they claim to have no knowledge of the reason behind their actions. But if a Black church moves out of the beaten path of White identification, White people feel very upset, very disturbed. If a professor on a Black college campus begins to teach anything other than accommodation to the White declaration of Black inferiority, White people feel immediately threatened and money begins to be cut off from that institution. All institutions in the Black community were established as mechanisms of control for Black people and to perpetuate the authority of the White power establishment. "Integration" is the name given to the Black man's philosophy of self-hate, and the dream of integration is the mechanism by which

Black people permit themselves to be controlled.

Black people in America are united by a bond of common experiences. We are not Americans in the sense that White people speak of being Americans. We fight in your wars. Your astronauts go to the moon. The wealth of America belongs to you. We are not Americans. We are Black people who against our will were brought to America. We are a people because here in America common experiences have welded us together as a people, and because we share a common background, and a common cultural heritage which is African in origin. Our cultural heritage has been mixed up, confused, and changed by our American experience, but it binds us together even when we would break apart. In one respect the White man was very kind. He said, "Any person who has any Black blood at all is Black!" So we don't have to worry about whether or not we are all Black or just a little bit Black. If we're Black at all, we're all Black, and so psychologically we share a common cultural heritage. The agony of being Black in America unites all Blacks with bonds which even self-hated cannot break. The White man's oppression drives us together even as we dream of integration with him. All Black people experience the same dehumanizing oppression, brutality, and second-class citizenship. No matter how learned a Black man may be, his children find it difficult to get a decent education in a public school. No matter how well-mannered he may be, he finds it difficult to secure a decent house to live in. These are the things which make a people, and so the Black experience has made us a people. Only a Black fool can believe that he is not discriminated against in America. The White man's declaration of Black inferiority has served to provide for Black people a unique experience. And our lives are the result of this Black experience. We have been shaped and molded by it. And so we are separate people. We can sit in the same room, we can live in the same town, we can be neighbors on the same street—but we're a different people because our experiences have been different.

So for a Black person, authority is a much different thing than it is for a White person. The very institutions you wish to preserve, we wish to destroy. When you react with hostility because your institutions have been attacked, we react with glee and with the desire to participate in their speedy destruction. When young White people march on the Pentagon, we cheer because they are attacking one of the institutions which oppress us. When hippies cry out that Western civilization must be

81

restructured because it is destroying mankind, we say amen. So the Black man is not a part of White America. We have been placed outside by the White man's declaration of Black inferiority. The Black liberation struggle has become the dominant expression of the Black experience, and it affects all aspects of our life. And that is not to say that you don't know a maid or a bellhop who will tell you that he is well satisfied with life in America. But more and more all Black people are being caught up in the liberation struggle.

It's very difficult now to find a Black person who is totally outside of the basic liberation struggle in which Black people are engaged. The Black church is moving slowly into the struggle, and it is my hope and prayer that the liberation struggle will soon become its heart and center, bringing a new stability, dynamic, and sense of direction. This will not be accomplished, however, without confrontation and conflict. Every Black institution must fight its way out of bondage to the White power establishment. Every Black college is being torn asunder by the efforts of Black students to bring the colleges into the liberation struggle. The ultimatum is simple: "Come into the struggle or we'll burn the college down." In every Black community

Black people are insisting that everything become a part of the Black liberation struggle, that there be no elements in the community that are separate and apart from the struggle. No businesses are to be permitted to remain in the community that are not a part of the Black community, and controlled by the Black community. We are engaged in an all-out struggle for Black liberation and more and more *this* determines the Black man's life.

The struggle is coming to determine everything about our existence. And this makes the Black man different and strange and difficult to understand. We are no longer a part of the things that trouble you, that you believe in. For us the church must become an institution which serves the interests of the Black community and the liberation struggle of Black people. We reject the mythology by which you have kept us enslaved by our faith in the authority of your pronouncements, your institutions, and White power establishment.

We believe that Jesus is a revelation of God, but not the only revelation. We believe that we have a revelation in Marcus Garvey who looked at the world in which Black men live and asked, "Where is the Black man's government?" and called Black men to build a Black nation in Africa. We have a revelation of God in Brother Malcolm who

83

taught Black people that the White man is an enemy and that you can't deal with an enemy in terms of persuasion. Because that's what Black people were doing when Brother Malcolm began to talk. Dr. King was organizing mass demonstrations across the South, and White people were showing day after day that in any situation in which the Black man appears to threaten White institutions, all White people will come together. But we needed Brother Malcolm to interpret the simple truth that the White man is an enemy. He revealed to us that the fact that we are dealing with an enemy structure and that even when White people say that they are liberal, they still hate Black people because they are partners in the White declaration of Black inferiority. Even though a White man lives in a community without a single Black person, he still shares in the benefits of a White society which derives much of its wealth from the exploitation of Black people. So all White people are a part of the exploitation, are a part of the whole process; and so it was very important for Brother Malcolm to tell Black people: "You're dealing with an enemy, and you deal with an enemy in a different way than you would with a friend." And that's where Black people find the demands of the liberation struggle difficult, because the authority of old master's pronouncements about turning the other cheek and going the second mile linger on.

Black people must understand that only within the Black nation do we turn the other cheek. We turn the other cheek only to a Black brother, or a Black sister. We do not turn the other cheek in any other situation, and it's my firm conviction that this is what Jesus was talking to Israel about in the first place, because Israel was engaged in the same kind of liberation struggle against the White Gentile world. The teachings of the Bible must be reinterpreted for the benefit of Black people so that the church can become useful in the liberation struggle. If the Black church cannot free itself from the White church, then the Black church will have to be destroyed by Black people, and we will have to find a new religion and build a new independent church resting upon the authority of the Black experience. Only if we can rediscover the historic roots of Christianity and strip from it the mystical distortions which are not basic to the concept of nation as revealed in the Old Testament and in the teachings of Jesus, will we be able to bring the Black Christian church into the liberation struggle and make it relevant to the lives of Black people.

So we face in the pews of the Black churches across America the same kind of unrest that you find in the White pews, but for a different reason. In the White pews White people are saying to White preachers, "Defend our institution." And Black people are saying to Black preachers, "Build our institution. Stop catering the White authority. Free yourself from the domination of the White institutionalism." And so we live in a very, very significant time when the church is being forced to change. The White church must change because White people in the pews are demanding that it defend the White institutional structure which has declared Black people inferior. The Black church must change because Black people are demanding that it become a part of the liberation struggle, that the church become the heart, soul, and brains of the liberation struggle, that it become a teaching church in the sense that it teaches Black people the things that are necessary if they are to participate intelligently in the liberation struggle, that it organize Black people effectively for participation in the liberation struggle, that it give Black people again a sense of dignity as children of God, God's chosen people.

It's becoming impossible for Black people to use Sunday school literature from White publishing houses. Literature from Black church publishing houses is just as bad because it's a copy of the same material. Such is the persistence of White authority. When White publishing houses began to put just enough Black pictures in every quarterly to make it "respectable," this did not change the basic White orientation of the literature. Black church school literature must teach Black children at all age levels that there is nothing more sacred than the liberation of Black people. This message can be conveyed in terms of the heroic biblical stories of the Old Testament, the heroism of Jesus, the heroism of Black men and women who have served the continuing struggle. The emphasis must be on the hero motif and the basic idea that there is nothing more sacred than the liberation of Black people. The idea of individualism must be rejected, and this must be emphasized over and over again. There is no reason to have a church school lesson in a Black church that does nothing to combat the individualism of the White world. Black children must come to realize that the communal life of Africa is the most desirable way of life for Black people and that this is the direction in which we must be moving. The individualism of the White man's society is death and destruction, and Black children must begin to realize that they can bury

87

their individualism in the life of the Black nation. Children must be taught that sacrifice for the Black nation is important. The death of individualism is necessary if Black people are to survive. The Black church, then, must undertake a total restructuring of the church and its educational functions. We must develop techniques which do not depend upon trained teachers. We must learn to use the mechanical techniques of tape recorders, filmstrips, and movies that can be sent out to small churches everywhere. Even without trained teachers they can carry the same basic message to Black people everywhere. We must become a people like the Black children of Israel as they stood on the plains of Moab ready to enter into the Promised Land. They had wandered for forty years in the wilderness, and they had learned to find their authority in their own experience. No longer did they bear the mark of slavery and dream of returning to bondage in Egypt. The King of Moab looked out upon the nation Israel, and said, "A people has come out of Egypt." Only if the Black church can build a Black people in America with the courage to stand against the repressions which are rising everywhere will Black people be able to survive.

If, then, we are moving toward a Black-White polarization and the Black church is moving toward

Black nationhood and the White church is moving to defend institutional White supremacy and repression, what hope do Black people have? White people have the preponderance of power, numbers, armies, ammunitions. What hope is there for Black people? It is a complex question and one which cannot be decided in terms of whether or not Black people can win an armed conflict. We do not have a choice. Having once decided to be free, a man cannot decide how free he wants to be. He knows that he is either free or he is a slave.

But White people also face a problem in a complex society such as this—how dangerous can a minority of twenty-five million people be in terms of the destruction of a society? Certainly, in Germany it was difficult to kill six million Jews, and they were docile and compliant. In America it would be very difficult to kill twenty-five million Black people without destroying America in the process.

There is, however, a state of human society which is not taught so often from the pulpit, namely, an equilibrium or balance between opposing forces. Black people are trying to build a nation and become a people to establish a balance of power sufficient to protect Black people against the oppression, exploitation, and brutality which the powerless

cannot escape in a White society which has declared all non-White people inferior. The Black
man must fight to escape from powerlessness even
though he die in the attempt.

The most an intelligent White man can hope
for in America is that this balance-of-power equilibrium shall come into being as quickly as possible.
Rational White people should be contributing to
the building of this equilibrium for reasons of self-
interest. If Black people are forced to remain
powerless, anger and frustration will be a constant
source of danger. If Black people could secure
sufficient power to maintain a balance which protects Black people against the White man's declaration of Black inferiority, it might be possible for
Black people and White people to live together
as two separate people in one country. Black people
will remain separate, using the separateness which
already exists as a basis for power rather than
permitting the White man to use it for exploitation
and oppression.

The separateness that Black people now have in
America is a basis for political power, for economic
power, and for the transmission of cultural values.
This separateness the Black church must nurture
because it is the basis upon which the Black man
can build a protective balance of power. The only

hope for peace in America depends upon the possibility of building this kind of Black power. Black people will not again passively accept slavery. A Black nation within a nation must come into being if we are to survive. For the Black man everything must be judged in terms of Black liberation. There is but one authority, and that is the Black experience.

THE LOCUS OF AUTHORITY: PARTICIPATORY DEMOCRACY IN THE AGE OF THE EXPERT

roger l. shinn

My title could just as well be inverted. It might read, "The Authority of the Expert in the Age of Participatory Democracy." The point is that contemporary society—all over the world and nowhere more than in the United States of America—faces a deep dilemma in its effort to locate authority. In this technological epoch with its intricate social structures, we human beings are more dependent than ever before upon experts with skills we do not share and barely comprehend. Yet, perhaps for that very reason, we are all the more resentful of these expert authorities, all the more insistent upon making decisions ourselves. My opinion is that nobody knows how the human race will work itself out of that dilemma. I have no solution for it; my aim is to define it, hopefully to clarify it, and to chip away a bit at it.

I. Two Types of Authority

The problem of authority appears in its most obvious form because every person lives in an environment both social and natural. He cannot behave in total subjective capriciousness. He butts up against a reality. He must adjust his conduct to the conduct of others and the demands of nature. He recognizes that he is subject to authority.

Two kinds of authority are immediately recognizable. The first can be called operational authority. The functioning of society requires that some decisions be made, that these be binding upon the society, and that they be to some extent enforceable. The second can be called noetic authority, using that term very broadly to include all apprehension of truth.[1] Life requires some recognition—often,

[1] In its strict sense noetic refers to intellectual activity. For convenience I am using the word loosely to refer to all human apprehension of truth, whether empirical, rational, or intuitive.

93

it seems a flimsy and corrupted acknowledgment, but some acknowledgment—of truth.

Operational authority comes from the necessity of a society, whether an immense national society or a small voluntary community, to develop some means of decision making. Sometimes it does not matter greatly who decides, so long as a decision is made. Those societies that are blessed or cursed with the automobile require traffic rules. In most countries traffic moves on the right side of the road; the British drive on the left. No doubt there can be endless minor arguments as to which style is preferable, but the important thing is that a decision be made. Without a decision total chaos and danger would replace the partial chaos and danger with which automobile-infatuated societies have learned to live. The big issue is not the truth or righteousness of leftward and rightward principles; on this issue Soviet Communists are rightists and British capitalists are leftists. All that matters is an expedient procedure. Whether the decision be made by plebiscite or by a centralized traffic control office is relatively inconsequential; in either case the driver is accountable to an authoritative decision.

In other cases of operational authority it matters greatly how the decision is made. Taxation is an example. Every society from the most primitive to the most sophisticated has methods by which its members are required to contribute something of personal services, goods, or money to the common economic burdens of the society. The procedures become imbedded in the folkways or the legislation of the society. The method is generally the outcome of some interplay among conflicting interests. The system that prevails is an expression of the power conflicts and power structures of the society, perhap modified by some overarching concern for the common good. Taxation is the usual method in societies that use money. Tax regulations have operational authority; despite chiseling and evasions, they are somewhat enforceable. Individuals or groups may resent them as contrary to their own interests; they may cry out to heaven that they are unfair; they may, in the name of self-interest or justice, defy or seek to change them. I am not presupposing that any given system of taxation is sacrosanct or just. I am only saying that society is inconceivable without some operational authority in this as in many other areas. To reject a given authority is to demand a better one, not to deny the need for operational authority.

The second type of authority, noetic authority, is quite different from the first. It derives less from the political process than from the nature of things.

Men do not enact the law of gravity and enforce it. They acknowledge it and learn to live with it. To defy it is to ask for disaster. To recognize it is to admit a certain subservience to it, then to learn both to accept it and to take advantage of it for human purposes. A skillful use of it, as in the construction and enjoyment of aircraft, may mean a qualified transcendence of it. Men today are far more successful than the mythical Icarus, not because they scorn the law but because they have learned techniques of working with it. Its authority remains unchallenged.

In modern times science has been the most spectacularly effective way of acquiring knowledge. It has often achieved an authority displacing sanctified authorities of the past. John Dewey once described its import in language deliberately parodying the book of Job: "Though this method slay my most cherished belief, yet will I trust it." [2] For Dewey the scientific method was accessible to everyone; that was one of its great virtues. But obviously science requires expert practitioners in a variety of specific disciplines. Hence, the scientist is able to speak in the area of his expertise with an authority lacking to other people. Technology,

[2] "Fundamentals," *The New Republic*, XXXVII (1924), p. 176.

related to, yet different from science, has its experts too. On many subjects each of us has to defer to the expert. Whatever virtues are claimed for free discussion, each of us is incompetent to discuss some questions. On many a topic my opinion is worthless. All I know, as Will Rogers used to say, is what I read in the papers—or see on television or find in a magazine or book. And much of the time I am then trusting the judgment of the expert.

If, in an enthusiasm for freedom of speech, I assert that the moon is made of green cheese, I may be exercising a constitutional right but not a moral or intellectual right. I am speaking without authority. If I say that the moon is made in part of iron and titanium, I am more credible. Technology enabled men to go to the moon and bring back some rocks; scientists found iron and titanium in the rocks. I have read that in the press. I can state the fact, not on my own authority, but with an echo of the authority of science. Conflicting interests are irrelevant to the question; no process of discussion or elections will affect the case. Sanity and intelligence require acceptance of the authority of the expert.

The two types of authority, operational and noetic, are decisively different. Operational authority is necessary for social functioning, even for

97

social existence. In cases of controversy, most of us will not yield up our judgment to an expert because our own interest is involved. Decisions must be made, often for the sake of survival, even though there may be no unanimity of judgment or even of the canons by which judgments should be made. We want to influence the judgments just as far as we can. Noetic authority in a very different way requires the judgment of those competent to assess the evidence and understand. Most of us will make judgments in the areas where we have expertise and will acknowledge the judgments of other experts elsewhere. Often, if evidence is inadequate, we can afford to wait a few days, a generation, or forever rather than make foolish and erroneous judgments.

Anybody who is not an utter fool will try to sift out the two kinds of authority—those on which he will pit his own authority against the world and those on which he will rely on experts to tell him what he does not know. But then he will quickly find that in human life, above all within a technological society, the two types of authority are usually intermingled. Effective operational decisions require expertise. And in this age of the knowledge explosion nobody is expert on all the issues he must meet.

If I travel on an airplane, I am abjectly dependent upon the expertise of a pilot, of men who design airports and navigational systems, of an industry that co-opts more skills than I can count to manufacture and service planes. If I simply stay home and drink a glass of water, I depend upon plumbers and engineers, upon chemists who know how much chlorine to put in the water, upon a giant technical and political system that defines watersheds, designates reservoirs, and gets tolerably drinkable water into cities. If I switch on an electric light, I rely on the know-how of building contractors and electricians, of legislators and inspectors, and of a vast industry of specialists. If I turn on the television set, my reliance is on an incredibly larger number of experts. In all these cases I am so utterly dependent that when on occasion the system lets me down, I can respond only with futile rage or laughter while I wait for somebody with authority to patch things together.

Yet, in every case I have an expertise lacking to the masters of the system. I know how the process affects me. I experience it directly, and I am an authority on its impact upon me. Although I would be a fool to tell the air pilot or the electronics engineer how to do his job, I would be equally a fool to assume on his authority that the whole process meets my needs. On these points where I am the authority, I use whatever political or economic clout I command to influence the system.

Suppose we carry the examples into the most controversial issues of public policy. An example is the national economy. How does the society move to maintain full employment, avoid inflationary exploitation of the vulnerable, distribute its goods and services with some kind of efficiency and equity, husband wisely its natural resources, and avoid disastrous pollution of its atmosphere and waterways? We are now doing a wretched job. Even the experts know too little about the whole intricate process, and they often disagree. Yet we need them. Without expertise this society cannot do the job; without authoritative knowledge the fumbling efforts of the best motivated people are likely to inflict harm on themselves and others.

A second example is hunger. The standard estimate is that ten thousand people die in this world every day from starvation and diseases connected with malnutrition. How do affluent Americans do something about that? By eating less and taxing themselves more? Possibly. But such measures may be futile gestures. The answer requires the expert knowledge of the best authorities on nutrition, on plant hybridization, on transportation of foods, and the economies of many nations. Men with the authority that derives from competence may tell us that in some countries there can be no answer to hunger without greater political stability, that elsewhere there can be no answer without revolution. Effective operational decision depends upon expert knowledge.

Thus, we, all of us, find ourselves dependent upon the expert authority who has knowledge we lack. But we do not therefore automatically trust the expert. We want to know what his purposes are, whom he serves, who pays him. We suspect that he may use his knowledge against our ignorance to expand his authority beyond his competence or to exploit us.

Let us assume that there are authorities, far less than omniscient but knowledgeable, on economic issues. We may ask how the economist heading the Federal Reserve Board translates his noetic authority into operational authority. How does he relate his expertise to the political forces that appointed him and to all of us? Why do economists hired by industry so often quarrel with those hired by labor unions? Why do those employed by the unions differ from those who speak for the unorganized poor? Can we be sure that any speak for the poor, who by definition are usually neither economists nor employers of economists?

Then, when we have asked all these questions, probably without getting adequate answers, we may ask another one. What does it do to human beings to become so dependent upon authority? The democratic ethos and the spirit of self-respect resist despotism, whether benevolent, cruel, or the falsely benevolent that is really cruel. Modern Western man, still living in the pride of victory over the despotisms of the past, sometimes wonders uncomfortably: Is he more beholden to authority than his ancestors, who knew that they were knuckling under to empire or church? Is this contemporary man, who elects public officials and exercises rights of free speech to berate them, actually the ignorant victim of authorities in science and industry, military technology, economics, sociology and psychology, government, and so on? How many citizens can follow with any expert judgment the complicated debates on armaments races, causes of crime, the generation gap, reasons for rising relief rolls, merits of ghetto schools, ecological effects of the automobile, causes and cures of cancer, safety of aircraft in crowded holding areas, benefits and risks of the pill, exhaustion of natural resources, social effects of tight monetary policy, prospects for genetic manipulation, and economics of medical care—to mention a few of the many issues that scream for attention today?

Each of us relies upon the authority of the expert at points important to his own well-being, and none of us trusts the expert entirely. "Is it 'inevitable' (or at least 'highly probable')," asks Harold Laswell, "that industrial societies will alienate the younger generation?" [3] Is it inevitable, I ask further that such societies alienate many people young and old? The suspicion spreads that the authority of the system is pitted against genuine human interests. That suspicion infiltrates groups who otherwise have little in common—angry populists who reject the major political parties and vote for George Wallace for president, bright university students from the second generation of affluent families, Black militants angry with a system that has not dealt them a share of the power. In no sense do I equate these three groups nor think their ideas of justice are the same. They are, however, similar in one way—their alienation from authority. They ask for a shake-up in power structures from which

[3] "Civil Education in the Technoscientific Age," in *Approaches to Education for Character*, ed. Clarence H. Faust and Jessica Feingold (New York: Columbia University Press, 1969), p. 33.

103

they feel excluded. They see somebody else constantly claiming authority and making decisions. Out of the demands for participation in the decision making comes the contemporary cry for participatory democracy.

II. Participatory Democracy and Elitism

Participatory democracy is a favorite current phrase of some groups who are alienated from established authority. It is especially the phrase of the New Left. By its very nature it is diverse and fluid, so it is not easy to characterize in terms of specific institutions or procedures. The name itself tells us something. It aspires to democracy rather than monarchy or aristocracy, whether in the family, the community, the university, or the large society. And it asks that the democracy be not merely representative but participatory; that is, it requires not simply that people elect representatives who make decisions but that everyone get into the decision making.

Frequently its rhetoric is revolutionary, and this rhetoric has had its influence, both in firing the resentments of those who are eager to condemn radicalism and in winning support from uneasy liberals who realize that they have conspired more than they realized with the system. As Stanley

Kaufmann of *The New Republic* puts it, "Revolutionary ideas of all kinds have become a new spectator sport for the increasingly affluent, increasingly educated, and therefore increasingly guilt-ridden (and guilt-enjoying) middle class." [4] Protestors, who lack many of the weapons of power, have proved skillful in exploiting this guilt. Even so, they have only rarely made an actually revolutionary effort. Robert Bendiner writes, "Today's left has less a program for revolutionary change than a fondness for using revolutionary rhetoric and tactics to extract immediate concessions from the Establishment." [5]

An examination of the meaning of authority in contemporary protest movements shows a curious dilemma. It is related to the distinction I have made between operational and noetic authority. From the magnificent premise that every person is valuable it sometimes moves to the dubious procedural conclusion that everyone's opinion is valuable on any subject. At this stage it attacks the authority of the expert, an authority that it easily shows to be frequently inflated or ideologically

[4] "Stanley Kaufmann on Films," *The New Republic,* December 21, 1968, p. 43.

[5] "Poverty Is a Tougher Problem Than Ever," *New York Times Magazine,* February 4, 1968, p. 71.

corrupted. In discrediting undue deference to authority, it sometimes discredits the whole idea of expert authority. A society that relies so largely as ours on expertise is thereby forced to ask, as it seldom has done, what is the legitimate function of expert authority.

At this point some kind of role assignment is in order. The old saying is that I know better than anybody else where my shoe pinches. That knowledge does not tell me how to make shoes. I must defer on that matter to the shoemaker. But I will not surrender my authority, grounded in experience of the pinch, to an expert maker or salesman of shoes. The shoemaker and I do not have the same authority, but each of us has an authority that the other must reckon with if I am to get comfortable shoes.

A more complex example, which is the center of intense controversy in our society, is medical practice. I know better than anyone else where I ache. That does not mean that I can prescribe the right medicine or surgery, least of all perform the surgery. In one sense my reliance upon authority is almost total. The physician knows a lot that I do not know. If he is mistaken, as doctors sometimes are, I still cannot be my own authority on the cure of any serious medical problem. If I come to distrust the judgment of one doctor, I will try another rather than go it alone. I quickly distrust the doctor who does not take me seriously and recognize that he is dependent upon me for information, as I am dependent upon him. In this sense I must participate in the healing process. Yet I participate as one who lacks needed knowledge and seeks authoritative judgment and skill.

Although I rely on the physician to provide a medical expertise that I lack, I do not maintain the same relationship when we discuss questions of medical economics. Some physicians do, in fact, try to extend their professional authority into this area, and it is not unknown for a medical organization to do the same. But I fight back when that happens. (I always prefer to fight physicians who are not treating me.) For two reasons I refuse to grant to the medical profession the same expertise in economic questions that I readily grant in medical questions. First, I think I know as much about economics as most physicians. Second, even if they know more than I, then I become all the more distrustful of their authority because I fear that they may use that economic knowledge for their advantage, not for mine. On questions of medical judgment the doctor's advantage is usually coincident with mine. Not always: When the American

Cancer Society provides expert medical testimony, tobacco companies can usually hire experts too; financial gain may not be unrelated to medical judgment. But I assume a greater coincidence of interest between doctor and patient on the gain of healing the patient than on the financing of medical care.

My conclusion is that participatory democracy cannot afford to neglect expert authority, but that such authority does not establish hierarchies of personal worth and does not erase the importance of personal mutuality. In a society so dependent upon expertise as ours, the tension over authority becomes critical. Established authorities err by exaggerating their authority, claiming to know what is good for people better than the people themselves, and using their authority to maintain their own prestige. Protestors retaliate by disdaining authority, even at those points where competent authority is necessary.

The general outlines of an answer are easy to suggest. It is desirable to keep all authority subject to criticism and to hold it accountable to public good. The implementation of the answer is far more difficult. On some questions the only adequate criticism is an informed criticism, and that may mean that criticism takes place only within the authoritative clan, which has an inherent defensiveness against outsiders. Hence, this problem is likely to be a persistent one in our society.

The advocates of participatory democracy face the issue, not only in opposition to entrenched authority, but also within their own movements. They frequently begin as egalitarians, then quickly become elitists. Thus, some student leftist movements claim to articulate the discontents of most students, as indeed they occasionally do. But if students in general do not share the goals of the leftists, then the leftists sometimes seek to manipulate or "radicalize" the sluggish student masses. Inept administrative authorities may help them. But very often in a subtle or not-so-subtle change participatory democracy gives way to arrogant elitism. This is particularly the case when radical leadership invokes revolutionary goals at a time when most people are not in a revolutionary mood. As political scientist Robert O'Brien has put it, "Most modern revolutions are not popular in leadership. The revolutionary situation exists and is exploited by the revolutionary elite." [6] In a genuinely revolutionary situation the gap between elitism and participatory democracy is not immense. If the situa-

[6] *War and/or Survival* (Garden City, New York: Doubleday & Co., 1969), p. 202.

tion is not authentically revolutionary or if most people do not experience it as such, then elitism may directly contradict participatory democracy.

Paul Goodman, usually known as a friend of the New Left, has pointed to the contradiction in rhetoric and practice between the two terms, *participatory democracy* and *cadres*. He endorses the first, but sees a menace in the second. As he traces the history of the Students for a Democractic Society, it began with an authentically democratic impulse, then too often turned into a "dictatorial" and "presumptuous manipulation of people for their own good." [7]

I find this issue a perplexing one because, more than Paul Goodman, I think that society usually moves only under the impulse of aggressive leadership which is in some sense elite, but which, I hope, need not be dictatorial and manipulative. Gordon Allport in his famous study of *The Nature of Prejudice* compares democratic methods of ending segregation with "strong and forthright action from 'higher up.'" In a White-dominated situation, discussion about the end of segregation may bring persistent resistance, whereas a strong act of leadership without preparatory discussion usually brings

[7] "The Black Flag of Anarchism," *New York Times Magazine,* July 14, 1968, pp. 10 ff.

"no more than a flurry of excitement of short dura-
tion." "The *fait accompli,*" he says, "is often welcomed if it is in line with one's conscience." [8]
Thus, he made the judgment in 1958 that "it
probably would have been psychologically sounder"
for the Supreme Court to have insisted upon
"prompt acquiescence" with its school desegregation
ruling of 1954 instead of asking compliance with
"deliberate speed," thereby permitting faltering
leadership and organization of opposition.[9] Probably most of us are sufficiently conditioned by the
language of democracy that, while we endorse desegregation, we prefer to believe that it comes more
effectively through democratic means than by
governmental *fait accompli.* Does Allport's judgment inevitably favor elitism over participatory
democracy? Not necessarily. He is not saying that
all kinds of behavior can be imposed from above.
He says that in a situation where many men are
involved in a struggle between prejudice and conscience, the imposed directive is likely to be effective

[8] (Anchor Books; Garden City, New York: Doubleday,
1958), pp. 262-63.

[9] *Ibid.,* p. v. The earlier citation from Allport (see note
8) comes from the book originally published in 1954 and
written prior to the Supreme Court decision. The comment
on the implementation of that decision comes from the 1958
preface to the paperback edition of the book.

if it supports conscience. He is not advocating that elites manipulate the population in accord with the private purposes of the elites.

Allport's qualification protects him from the dangerous elitism of Herbert Marcuse, who for a time exercised great fascination over the New Left. Marcuse has candidly advocated "withdrawal of toleration of speech and assembly from groups and movements which promote aggressive policies, armament, chauvinism, discrimination on the grounds of race and religion, or which oppose the extension of public services, social security, medical care, etc." [10] He grants that this would mean the imposition of the will of a small elite upon society, and he justifies it because he thinks we live in a time of "clear and present danger." He seems scarcely aware that his form of leftist philosophy is on this issue a mirror image of rightist repression-ary movements that would deny him the right to speak. And he seems quite unaware that he is advocating a kind of neo-Puritanism in which "the elect" impose their will upon the unregenerate.

III. The Agony of Democracy

The agony of democracy in our time arises not only out of honest perplexity over the authority of

[10] "Repressive Tolerance," in *A Critique of Pure Tolerance* by Robert Paul Wolff (Boston: Beacon Press, 1965), p. 100.

the expert in a society that hopefully ascribes equal dignity to all men; it arises also out of the indifference of most men to injustices that they do not themselves feel. In such a situation the common slogans of our time, slogans that often express deep feelings of men, turn out to be inept clichés for meeting the crises of operational authority.

One such slogan, "majority rule" with "one man, one vote," has had a glorious history in times when minorities oppressed majorities. It turns out to be unhelpful when majorities are oppressing minorities. If eighty percent of the population systematically victimize and outvote twenty percent, the twenty percent will become cynical about the authority of the majority. Sociologist Herbert Gans has recently argued that this nation will never meet the needs of its poor and its Black citizens by reliance upon majority rule. Contented majorities can always outvote their victims. Hence he advocates a pluralistic democracy that makes deliberate efforts to include minorities in the political structure and to restrict majority rule. But he quickly grants that his idea is easier to hope for than to describe in detail and implement.[11]

[11] "We Won't End the Urban Crisis Until We End 'Majority Rule,'" *New York Times Magazine,* August 3, 1969, pp. 12 ff.

A second slogan, "self-determination," is one popular response to discontent with majority rule. It is a powerful expression of the aspirations of people tired of being shoved around. But as a standard of procedural authority it is extremely vague. In urban society—perhaps in all societies, but most obviously in megalopolis—everybody gets shoved around. Total self-determination is nonsensical. Imagine a society, for example, in which everybody determined for himself what taxes he would pay, how he would drive a car, or what laws he would obey. Human dignity cannot depend upon an impossible self-determination. It may demand that some areas of life be kept free from external coercion. And it may demand a relocation of operational authority so that some people do not exercise a high degree of self-determination that they deny to others.

A third slogan, "local control," is especially paradoxical. Governor Lester Maddox of Georgia has called for "local control of public education," in words remarkably similar to those used by Black leaders in Northern urban ghettoes. There is an immense difference in the motives. Governor Maddox, in my judgment, wants local control in order to perpetuate injustices that Whites have perpetrated against Blacks. The ghetto-dwellers want

114

local control in order to get out from under long injustices. The difference is a warning that "local control," like all other slogans, is not self-validating. As a principle for shifting operational authority, it may promote injustice or justice.

The turmoil of democracy in technological societies is likely to be with us for some time to come. None of the traditional systems of operational authority is working very well. People, seeking some power to direct their lives, run into constant double frustration. First, to choose wisely on most issues they must rely upon the authority of experts who know about complex topics that most people do not understand; yet they are justifiably reluctant to turn over momentous decisions to experts who are not accountable to the common good. Second, society includes many conflicting groups, whose peculiar interests do not obviously and readily cohere in a common good; and such traditional ways of adjudicating interests as majority rule, self-determination, and local control all have severe limitations.

Hence, many thinkers in these days are hoping for social inventions, perhaps related to new modes of communication, that will mean some breakthrough in the location of operational authority, some advance comparable to the invention of parliamentary democracy in a past age. Some such inventions, unforeseeable now, may ease the agony of democracy, expecially if they produce experts who adequately represent and remain accountable to the people who are not expert and have in the past not had access to experts. But social inventions, helpful though they may be, are not likely to remove the basic conflicts inherent in social life, any more successfully with these conflicts than we have done thus far.

IV. Theological Authority

The foregoing reflections have their significance for theological authority, which with all other forms of authority is experiencing its own time of troubles. Theological authority is essentially noetic rather than procedural; that is, theology seeks to be the *logos* of faith, the response to truthful revelation of God and man. For example, it is concerned with justice, not merely as the ideology of an interest group, but as a claim on and promise to all men. This noetic authority may become a guide to procedural authority, as a church makes organized efforts to live out its comprehension of faith and ethics.

In many ways the language I have used to analyze authority is peculiarly inappropriate to

116

theology. Can anyone talk about experts on the will and ways of God, about elites in the comprehension of the gospel of Christ? This very gospel confounds the usual notions of authority and expertise. The Apostle Paul affronted the whole authority structure of his time with his declaration: "God chose what is foolish in the world to shame the wise, God chose what is weak in the world to shame the strong, God chose what is low and despised in the world, even things that are not, to bring to nothing things that are, so that no human being might boast in the presence of God" (Rom. 1:27-29).

But if this gospel of Christ upsets the usual canons of authority, it begins to define some of its own. And as it does so, it meets problems not entirely dissimilar to those of other types of knowledge. That theology should be immune to the perplexities that haunt other human inquiries is an improbability that can be affirmed only in a crude theological arrogance.

Certainly Christian ideas of authority have never assumed that truth is most likely to come from majorities. The Christ who astonished the crowds because "he taught them as one who had authority, and not as their scribes" (Matt. 7:29) was the Christ who was crucified. The authority of his

117

voice and the power of his crucifixion are integrally related. Had he not been faithful unto death, few would have remembered his words of life. His followers recognized his authority, not because he met their preconceived criteria for authority but because he changed them.

Then they had to live with the change, and to this day they are not sure how to live with it. They came to regard themselves as "servants of Christ and stewards of the mysteries of God" (1 Cor. 4:1), as sharers in Christ's "ministry of reconciliation" (2 Cor. 5:18). Therein they faced a dilemma. Were they to be custodians of his truth, guardians against the perversions and distortions of it that constantly appear among men who would appropriate it for ends contrary to Christ's purpose? This response led to the definition of a canon, to warnings against heresy, to institutionalization of authority. Or were they to be faithful to Christ in his task of upsetting received tradition and established authorities, in his daring in opposing hierarchies and moving outside routinized channels? This response led to innovation, to the recognition of truth in unexpected sources, sometimes to the defiance of the very institutions that grew out of the first response.

The first impulse led to the enshrining of

authority in an infallible scripture, an infallible papacy, or an inviolate intellectual system, or institutional polity purportedly able to determine truth. The second impulse led to the confidence of enthusiasts able to rebel against authority because they claimed the truth, perhaps as dogmatically as the authorities they attacked. The excesses and distortions of either impulse do not refute the impulse itself, and neither impulse destroys the other.

Our epoch is thoroughly familiar with the erosion of traditional authority. Walter Lippmann has well described the "feeling" of modern men "that almost nothing they think today about social, political and worldly morals is sure to be valid in 30 years." [12] In such a time men are likely to side with Pascal who, in his controversy with the Jesuits, rejected the structures of authority and established his own authority simply in "the necessity of speaking." [13] Christians these days are less likely to be impressed by the erudite scholar who sifts the evidence to learn more about the historical Jesus than by the prophetic spokesman who announces what God is doing in history now.

[12] "The New American Role," *New York Post*, May 18, 1968, p. 8.
[13] *Pensées* (New York: Dutton, 1908), fr. 919.

Yet the stark either-or is certainly too naïve. Not everyone who feels the necessity of speaking is worth listening to, as anybody who has suffered through a filibuster knows. And not everyone who claims knowledge of God's ways is believable. Somehow the Christian community must maintain fidelity to the God known in past biblical history and to the same God who acts today. It lives by memory and expectation, including expectation of the unexpected.

There can be in Christian faith no authority that does not either arise out of human experience or somehow enter into that experience. Yet the whole message of the cross is that authority in some way stands over against us and our experience— especially the experiences that we are likely to assert most dogmatically and confidently. There are no experts in faith in anything like the sense that there are experts in chemistry or law or electronics. The elite, if we can use that word at all, are those to whom a grace is given; we call them prophets and apostles, and they usually upset men's expectations. So we come to a paradox. In one sense the community of faith must be suspicious of democracy; truth is not determined by majorities, and leaders of the community must often prod and affront reluctant constituencies, even when those constituencies have elected them. But in another sense this community must embrace participatory democracy with a peculiar passion—not with the assurance that discussion always leads to truth, but with the sensitivity that the word of truth may come from unexpected sources.

The word, when it comes, is less likely to bring a new hypothesis or body of data than a new perception of things, requiring men to reorder their previous perceptions. In that reordering the prophet and apostle do not have the sole authority. The entire community must relate its new perceptions to those perceptions centering in Christ. Its scholars and its agents must relate its present to its heritage, must probe the relation of the perceptions of faith to the understandings of the world opened up by science, must ask the meaning of faith for social policy in an intricately constituted society. Here the community needs the expertise of historians, philosophers and theologians, social scientists, strategist of action. Their role is not a haughty one, but it is indispensable.

The roots of Christian authority are double. One root digs deep into past history and appropriates, as our predecessors in the faith could say, "that which we have seen with our eyes, which we have looked upon and touched with our hands, concern-

121

ing the word of life" (1 John 1:1). The other root draws nourishment from a promise: "When the Spirit of truth comes, he will guide you into all the truth" (John 16:13). Interacting with these roots are the whole flowering structure of empirical and rational skills of secular man, skills that the community of faith believes are also of God. In this relationship of mutual sustenance there is an authority, ever living, adaptable, not wholly predictable, yet so compelling that the community can betray it only at the cost of its whole life and being. For this community it is the authority of the way, the truth, and the life. The continuous redefinition of its meaning is the work of every generation, not least of our own.

SELECTED BIBLIOGRAPHY

American Society for Political and Legal Philosophy. *Authority*. ed. Carl J. Friedrich, Cambridge: Harvard University Press, 1958.

————. *Justice*. ed. Carl J. Friedrich and John W. Chapman. New York: Atherton Press, 1963.

————. *Liberty*. ed. Carl J. Friedrich. New York: Atherton Press, 1962.

Aulén, Gustaf E. H. *Reformation and Catholicity*. Philadelphia: Muhlenberg Press, 1961.

Barth, Karl. *From Rousseau to Ritschl*, trans. Brian Cozens. London: S.C.M. Press, 1959.

Butler, Basil Christopher. *The Church and Infallibility*. New York: Sheed & Ward, 1954.

Collins, J. Henry. *Basis and Belief*. London: Epworth Press, 1964.

123

Cragg, Gerald R. *Reason and Authority in the Eighteenth Century*. Cambridge: The University Press, 1964.

Davies, Rupert Eric. *Religious Authority in an Age of Doubt*. Naperville, Ill.: Allenson, 1968.

Forsyth, Peter T. *Principle of Authority*. 2nd ed. Naperville, Ill.: Allenson, 1952.

Friedrich, Carl J. *Transcendent Justice: The Religious Dimension of Constitutionalism*. Durham, N. C.: Duke University Press, 1964.

Hanson, Richard P. *Tradition in the Early Church*. Philadelphia: Westminster Press, 1963.

Jenkins, D. E. *Guide to the Debate About God*. Philadelphia: Westminster Press, 1966.

Küng, Hans. *Structures of the Church*. Notre Dame, Ind.: University of Notre Dame Press, 1968.

Maritain, Jacques. *Man and the State*. Chicago: University of Chicago Press, 1951.

McKenzie, John L. *Authority in the Church*. New York: Sheed & Ward, 1966.

Mitchell, Wesley C., *et al. Authority and the Individual*. Cambridge: Harvard University Press, 1937.

Morrison, K. F. *Tradition and Authority in the Western Church, 300–1140*. Princeton: Princeton University Press, 1969.

Rahner, Karl. *Free Speech in the Church*. New York: Sheed & Ward, 1959.

Rokeach, Milton. *The Open and Closed Mind*. New York: Basic Books, 1960.

Shuster, George N., ed. *Freedom and Authority in the West.* Notre Dame, Ind.: University of Notre Dame Press, 1967.

Simon, Yves R. *A General Theory of Authority.* Notre Dame, Ind.: University of Notre Dame, 1962.

_____. *Freedom and Community.* ed. Charles P. O'Donnell. New York: Fordham University Press, 1968.

Todd, John M. *Problems of Authority.* Baltimore: Helicon Press, 1962.

Williams, Ronald, *et al. Authority and the Church.* Naperville, Ill.: Allenson, 1965.

Yarnold, G. D. *By What Authority?* London: Mowbray, 1964.

CONTRIBUTORS

Albert Buford Cleage, Jr., pastor of the Central United Church of Christ, Shrine of the Black Madonna, Detroit. An acknowledged leader in the Black revolution, subject of the biography by Hiley H. Ward, *Prophet of the Black Nation*. Author of the controversial book, *The Black Messiah*.

John L. McKenzie, S.J., Biblical scholar and Professor of Theology, University of Notre Dame. Author of *The Two-Edged Sword, Myths and Realities, The Power and the Wisdom, Dictionary of the Bible, Authority in the Church,*

The World of the Judges, The Roman Catholic Church, and *Second Isaiah.*

Clyde L. Manschreck, Professor of the History of Christianity, and Director of the Center for Reformation and Free Church Studies, Chicago Theological Seminary. Author of *Melanchthon: The Quiet Reformer, The Reformation and Protestantism Today, Prayers of the Reformers, A History of Christianity, Melanchthon on Christian Doctrine,* and *We Have This Heritage.*

Roger Lincoln Shinn, Dean of Instruction and William E. Dodge, Jr. Professor of Applied Christianity, Union Theological Seminary, New York. Author of *Beyond This Darkness, Christianity and the Problem of History, The Sermon on the Mount, The Existentialist Posture, Moments of Truth, Tangled World,* and *Man: The New Humanism.*